Jay Goldner has, without a d _____ ok
that could open the way to m _____ ad
our thinking into a different _____ the
very clear and exciting evide _____ and
reader-friendly voice, and _____ and
photographs of mysterious crop _____ uth-
seekers and skeptics alike. I dare you to read this book _____ , and
then not be convinced that extraterrestrials are attempting to communicate with us!

— Elizabeth English
Founder & Executive Director
Moondance International Film Festival

This book offers its readers a volume rich in text and illustrations, and Goldner's
remarkable hypotheses present the irrefutable possibility that we have, indeed, been
receiving communications from extraterrestrials. It is an invaluable resource of
information for those with even a passing interest in the subject. And for you
hardcore disbelievers, I believe this book may just open your eyes.

— Michael Edwards, Entertainment Showcase,
Lantern Light Productions

Jay Goldner has brought forth well-researched and well-documented facts about crop
circles that will leave you believing.

— Lance Carter
Host of the Radio Show, "Cinema Classics"

If Goldner is correct in his interpretation of the Chilbolton phenomena,
then he may go down in history as the man who first made large numbers
of people aware that we are now in touch with an extraterrestrial civilization.

— from the Foreword by Colin Wilson
Best-Selling Author, The Outsider, Alien Dawn

The truth is in here.
— Chris Chang
Managing Editor, Film Comment magazine

MESSAGES FROM SPACE

CROP CIRCLES BRING THE FIRST INDISPUTABLE EXTRATERRESTRIAL
SIGNS FROM SPACE

JAY GOLDNER

Published by Michael Wiese Productions
11288 Ventura Blvd., Suite 621
Studio City, CA 91604
tel. (818) 379-8799
fax (818) 986-3408
mw@mwp.com
www.mwp.com

Cover design:
Book layout: Gina Mansfield
Editor: Brett Jay Markel

Printed by Millbrook Printing Company
Manufactured in the United States of America

© 2002 Jay Goldner

The original edition of this book was published by
Verlag Die Silberschnur GmbH, Germany. © February 2002

Library of Congress Cataloging-in-Publication Data

Goldner, Jay, 1950-
Messages from space : crop circles bring the first indisputable
extraterrestrial signs from space / by Jay Goldner.
     p. cm.
     ISBN 0-941188-48-5
1. Human-alien encounters. 2. Crop circles—Miscellanea. I.
Title.
     BF2050 .G66 2002
     01.942—dc10
     2002010576

Photo Credits:
Steve Alexander: 12, 47, 50, 59, 61. 62; Colin Andrews: 114; Ken
Bakeman: 51, 84; Francine Blake: 12, 26, 39, 41, 111, 113; BLT
Research: 20; Toni Caldicott: 23; CLRC: 30-31; Cornell University:
12, 17; Zef Damen: 55, 57; Stuart Dike: 54, 129; Eric Eyler: 22;
Julian Gibsone: 39; Jay Goldner: 17, 42, 105, 55, 60, 63, 67, 72-
78, 83-84, 108, 116, 118-119, 123, 91; Charles R. Henry: 128;
Buddha & Laura Knight-Jadczyk: 65, Kurt Jonach: 62, Andrew
King: 23, 104, Ulrich Kox: 2, 21, 60, 61, Jürgen Krönig: 22,
Emanuel Kudris: 92, Charles R. Mallett: 36-37, 40, 65, 73, 100,
NASA: 66-68, 70-71, 86-88, 93, Lucy Pringle: 9, 14, 23-27, 32,
37-40, 46, 48, 57, 80, 83, 88, 92, 96-98, 107, Bruce A. Rawles:
104, 109, SETI: 93-95, Freddy Silva: 18, 38, 46, 51, 82, Peter
Sorensen: 47, 63, 114, Robert Speight: 37, 49, Studio Phoenix -
Archive: 12, 28-29, 31, 45-46, 51, 53, 54, 64, 69, 75-78, 81-82,
89, 91, 95, 99, 103, 106, 110-111, 114, 119, 121-122, 125,
130, Phillippa Coxall: 112, Steve Wingate: 70, 71.

As for the "pixel" reply to the Arecibo transmission, I think that anyone who studies it closely would agree that it would have taken a group of crop hoaxers armed with strings and some "corn-flattening" device many hours of hard work — always with the knowledge that they could easily attract attention or be noticed from the Chilbolton Observatory. If SETI wants to convince the world that it is a hoax, then all they have to do is to duplicate the feat in a single night.

It is the view of the author of this book, Jay Goldner, that the crop circles are formed more-or-less instantaneously, with some kind of energy beam in which the pattern is already encoded.

Goldner is not actually a crop-circle investigator. In reply to my queries, he explained that he is an Austrian who describes himself as an artist and illustrator who is also a part-time scientist. He has a deep interest in the paranormal, having been married to a wife who was a medium. (She "channeled" no less than three books by Jung, and both she and Goldner have lectured widely about these in America.)

Mr. Goldner is an admirer of the psychiatrist Wilhelm Reich (about whom I have also written a book), and runs a Reich archive. He was also a furniture designer, establishing a company that today employs 150 people.

If he is correct in his interpretation of the Chilbolton phenomena, then he may go down in history as the man who first made large numbers of people aware that we are now in touch with an extraterrestrial civilization — in which case, it seems likely that the Chilbolton glyphs are the prelude to a new epoch in human history.

PREFACE

"Crop circles" and "crop signs" are probably the most striking phenomena of cosmic inter-relationships we on earth have ever seen. No other modern wonder could make such an impression. To use the living fabric of nature as a huge "screen" on which to imprint intelligent messages is a pure act of genius, impossible to ignore.

The mandalas and other geometric or organic figures, which have appeared year after year in progressively more complex patterns, have understandably caused a worldwide controversy.

On the one side are the journalists of the mass media, who ignore the obvious and bathe in cynicism, perhaps suppressing their own subconscious fears. On the other side stand the alternative researchers, artists, and unorthodox scientists who are open-minded toward these phenomena. Regardless, most people have been swayed by neither side, remaining uninterested.

Even if about 20% of the crop figures are considered as pranks, this does not detract from the wonderfully exalted art of the remaining 80% ingeniously computed and exactly executed mathematical pictograms. Many of these must be viewed as symbols. In fact, the authentic crop-circle artists are taking great pains to show us what we on Earth need, whether on a scientific or a spiritual level — or a mixture of both.

My analysis will occupy itself primarily with the more concrete communications received from our cosmic artist friends. I will summarize all the symbolically coded content deciphered by half a dozen researchers, adding to them a number of interesting new findings and hypotheses of my own — some discovered only while working on this American edition.

I see these circles as stepping stones which may well have to be reinterpreted with each season, as an unseen hand surpasses the previous season's works of art in grain.

— Jay Goldner
August 2002

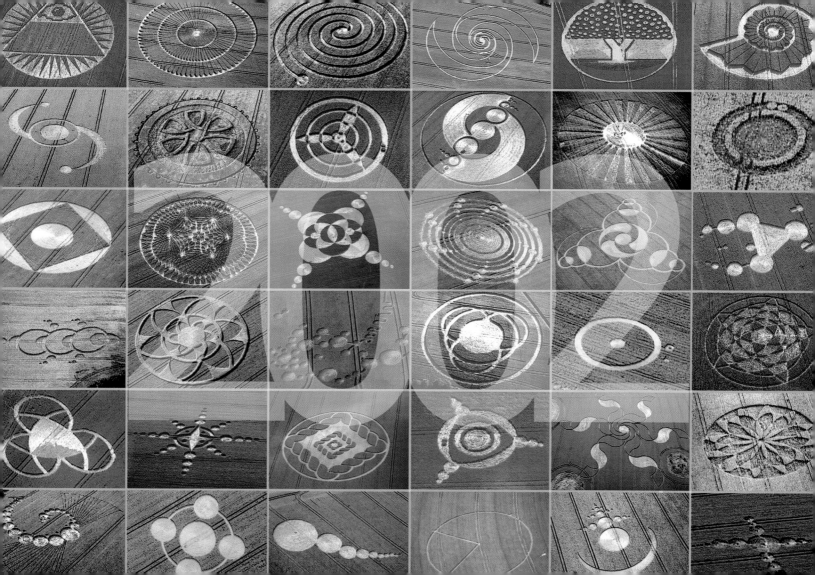

1974: OUR MESSAGE INTO SPACE

Arecibo, home of the world's largest radio-telescope, lies in the tropical jungle on the northern coast of Puerto Rico. Radio astronomy uses radio frequencies emitted by objects in space. As these signals are extremely weak, an ultra-sensitive reflector is needed. This is supplied at Arecibo by a huge aluminum dish which covers an area of 26 football fields. 123 yards above the 1000-foot diameter dish hangs a 75-ton dome. A 700-ton triangular platform suspended from cables is used to position the dome.

The Arecibo Observatory was built near the Equator (at 18°21' N and 66°45' E) because that location provides a highly interesting "slice" of the sky to be observed with its immovable 20° reflector. This jumbo instrument can transmit waves from 50 to 10,000 megahertz (i.e., wave-lengths between 1 foot and 5-1/2 yards).

As an initial test in 1974, the predecessors of the SETI (Search for Extra Terrestrial Intelligence) organization decided to send a coded message into space. The group chose as its target the cluster Messier 13 (M13) in "Hercules," a constellation close to 24,000 light-years away, with approximately 300,000 suns.

The signal group was sent on November 16, 1974, at 17:00 GMT. It was composed of 1679 impulses, which took only three minutes to send at two frequencies on the 2380 megahertz bandwith.

There are mathematical reasons for these impulses and frequencies. It was considered that any intelligent interstellar life form would understand us best by means of unique, significant universals and, in fact, would be looking for such universals!

As a result, SETI's Dr. Frank Drake, together with the astronomer Carl Sagan, chose the prime numbers 23 and 73 to form a matrix of the 1679 units. Because we as earth-dwellers cannot take for granted that other types of intelligent beings — ETs, aliens, or whatever we choose to call them — would understand human measurement units, it was most compelling to pack the matrix in the simplest of all forms: in the binary 0/1 code used in all computers. In this way the stream of 1679 impulses could be put into a single meaningful matrix, even by extraterrestrials.

The presumption is that an extraterrestrial civilization which is intelligent enough to communicate — in whatever way — will also know the number zero. Furthermore, such an intelligence will first try to divide the total by whole numbers. They will then discover that this is only possible, in SETI's message, with the numbers 23 and 73, which are prime numbers. And the next simple step will lead almost automatically to the conclusion that the row of signals must be embedded in a matrix!

In other words, if the signals sent by the Arecibo telescope reach an intelligent being, that being will be able to read and interpret them. (More on the mathematics of the SETI message can be found in the Appendix, page 101.)

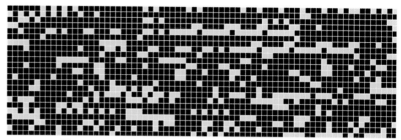
The series of impulses is not meaningful in horizontal order.

The dome houses a system of reflectors which focus radio waves picked up by the telescope's dish.

The world's largest telescope reflector has a diameter of 278 yards. The dome is marked with dashed box.

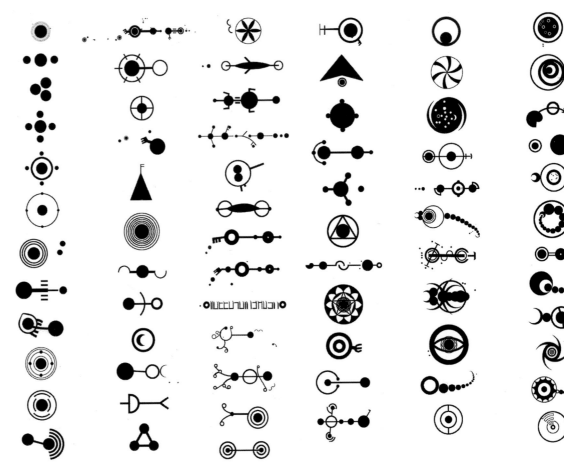

A COLLECTION
FROM THE
BEGINNINGS
OF THE
CROP CIRCLES

18

The first circles began to arouse attention in the late 1970s and early 1980s. In the beginning, they had simple forms, generally only circular spaces and rows of bent stalks of grain in English fields.

But then there were more and more mysterious crop graffiti, their forms no longer limited to single circles and/or simple combinations of lines. Now the formations were more complex symmetrical patterns, often featuring a long, pole-like character.

The formations were not unnoticed, with one particular theory taking hold: Spaceships (visible or invisible) had flown over the fields and somehow beamed the signs from the air. In fact, no one had a reasonable explanation for the phenomenon.

While the farmers whose fields were involved were annoyed at what they viewed as vandalism, small groups of researchers began to study these incidents, measure the artworks, and develop the first scientific theories about them.

Especially notable was the fact that the stalks of the plants involved were often not broken but only bent — as if by a gentle invisible hand.

The fans began to catalog the growing number of observations. Measuring standards were systematized and scientific methods standardized, but there were no real explanations for the occurrences.

The spectacle repeated itself every year in late spring and summer. A thriving tourist trade began to develop as more and more sightseers inspected the crop fields. Pubs established themselves as informal meeting places for what became known as the "Circle-Trekkies" and night-watch groups.

There were plenty of hypotheses: from mating dances of hedgehogs to intelligent wind-movements to UFO landing markers. Explanations not conforming to accepted scientific knowledge were dismissed out-of-hand, especially by a skeptical — and sometimes antagonistic — press.

Much of the press, specifically the British newspapers and Germany's *Der Spiegel*, declared the circles were the work of the infamous pranksters, Doug and Dave. And, indeed, there were some crop graffiti that were certainly the work of pranksters. But imitations were easily distinguished from genuine crop circles. To mark off a field geometrically and beat down some grain according to a certain pattern is not that difficult. But no imitator has been able to bend and not break the stems or to induce extended electromagnetic anomalies (where the measurements of energy inside and outside the circles differ greatly). And anyway, as the patterns became more complex, the possibility of pranksters became more unlikely.

The question "how" is hard enough to answer, considering that most of the circles and the signs develop at night or even in daylight without regard to whether the grain is green or ripe, wet or dry. The question "why" is considerably more difficult. Yet if we know the answer to the latter, the former would be easier to resolve. Until now, no one has been able to establish scientifically what powers are at the root of these occurrences.

Often the stalks of grain are bent and not broken.

The evolution of the "Agriglyphs," which is a more honorable name for the circles, has experienced an exponential growth: Every summer there are even more complex forms than the year before, mathematically aesthetic formations of supernatural beauty that turn up in scores in the midst of nature's galleries.

As the artistry improves, finer and finer nuances are added to the pictures. And their dimensions are increasing greatly, sometimes up to several hundred feet in size. A sort of alphabet of crop hieroglyphs has been collected, for the most part yet to be decoded.

Almost 10,000 different circles and signs, or close to 3500 formations (if you count them as groups), have been reported since the beginning of the phenomenon in an ever-expanding area around the world. If there is no grain available, then ice-fields or steppe landscapes have been found to carry the messages.

We can concentrate on the techniques: Do the anonymous artists use intelligent plasma-vortex rays or some other advanced technology? But this question seems more important: What kind of mental powers are able to so eloquently control these superior natural laws? Whoever possesses such creative potential must have good reason to send messages in this specific way.

The fact that the crop circles often refer to psychic changes makes it probable that the source is to some degree inspired by spiritual motives. The observations of light apparitions, but of no other visually perceptible signs, speak for the thesis that the effects even come from a different dimension. And it seems apparent that UFOs, ESP-experiences, and crop-imprinted circles are all somehow connected.

The facts collected over the last decade point more and more to a highly developed alien but friendly intelligence, dwelling somewhere in space around us. We may anticipate that it is only a matter of years to get into closer contact with that source.

The first major steps in that vision becoming a reality occurred in the summer of 2001.

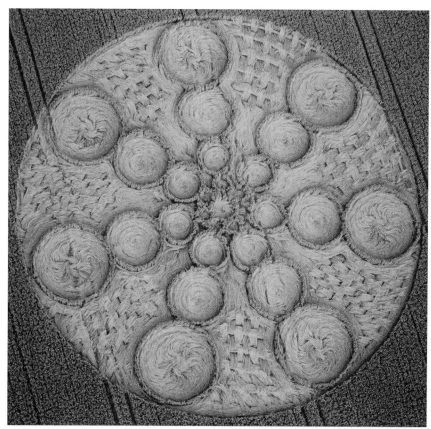

"The Basket" appeared near Bishop Cannings in 1999. It existed for only a few hours in the early morning before it was harvested.

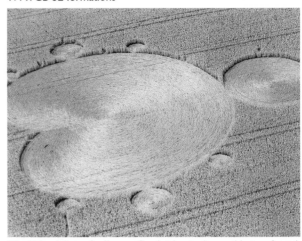

The "Mandelbrot Set," near Cambridge, is discernible in a fractal picture only calculable by computer.

The beginning of the crop circles is not well documented, but we do know that simple circles were found in the mid-70s. In the 1980s more complex diagrams were seen in southern England.

1990: The "Sri Yantra" was in a dry lake in Oregon (line lengths: 15-1/2 miles).

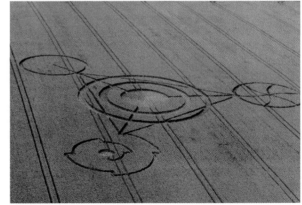

The "Barbury Castle Glyph" is considered the "mother of all pictograms."

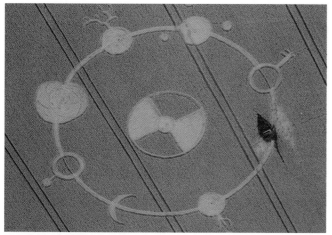

The "Dharma Wheel" of Silbury Hill has a large symbolic circle with a diameter of 45 yards.

The "Bythorn-Mandala" was discovered during this slow period for crop circles.

23

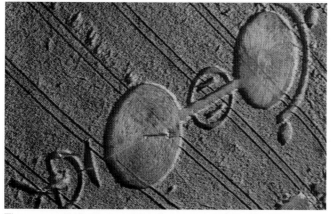

The seemingly "Sumeric symbols" were revealed in East Meon.

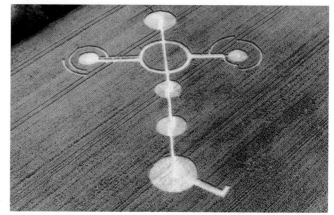

The giant "Cross formation of Loughborough" was remarkable.

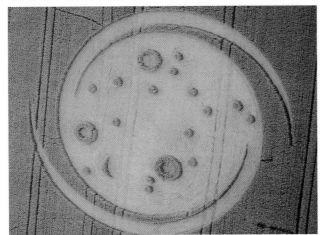

The "Galaxy" of West Stowell

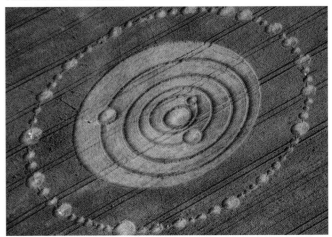

The "Solar System" of Longwood had an 88 yard-wide "asteroid belt," containing 65 circles.

The "Cobweb" of Avebury had a diameter of 300 feet.

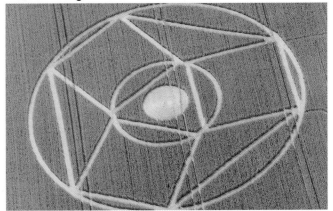

The "Sacred Geometry" pictogram of Winterbourne, with a 50-yard diameter, was a masterwork of simplicity.

The fractal "Julia-Set" of Windmill Hill, containing 149 circles, was a tremendous 305 yards in diameter.

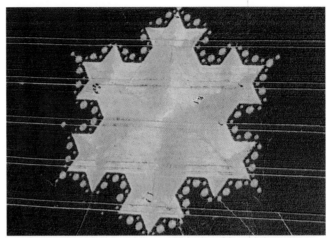

The fractal "Snowflake" of Silbury Hill had an 80-yard diameter.

The six-petaled "Oliver's Castle" design became famous because a video documented white balls flying above the field.

The two "Cresent Moons" of Oliver's Castle are also known as "Waterbug."

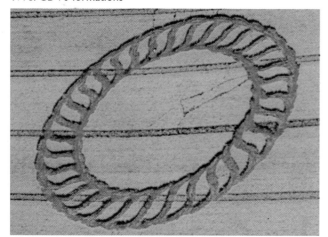

The "Beltane Wheel" had 33 flames.

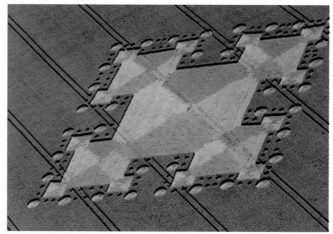

The precise "5 Pyramids" of East Kennet had a width of 110 yards and contained 156 circles.

The perfect "Septagon of Alton Barnes" had an area of 7,176 square yards.

The complex "Saros Cycle" was composed of the umbrae of total eclipses.

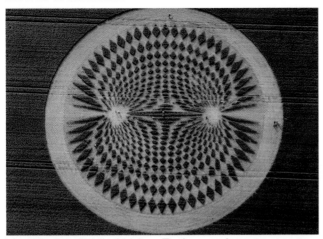

The "Magnetic Field" of Avebury Trusloe was the main attraction of the year.

The complex "3-circle-Vesica-Pisces" design of Liddington Castle

The "Hexa-Penta-Star" was found in Overton.

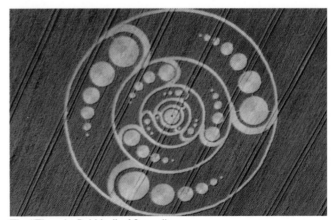

The "Thought Bubbles" of Stowell

27

An estimated 70-80% of all circles and symbols have appeared in England. They have been especially frequent in the southern counties Wiltshire and Hampshire, often believed to be a result of the special energetic constellation of this area. It is no coincidence that the world-famous stone circle of Stonehenge is also found here.

GREAT BRITAIN — MOTHER COUNTRY OF THE CIRCLES

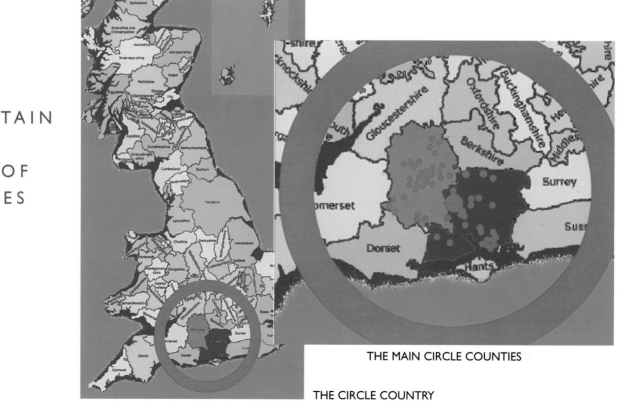

THE MAIN CIRCLE COUNTIES

THE CIRCLE COUNTRY

EUROPE
Belgium, Bulgaria, Denmark, Germany,
Finland, France, Russia, Ireland, Italy, Croatia,
Latvia, Netherlands, Norway, Austria, Poland,
Rumania, Sweden, Switzerland, Slovakia,
Slovenia, Spain, Czech Republic, Turkey,
Hungary

NORTH & SOUTH AMERICA
Brazil, Canada, Mexico, Peru, Puerto Rico, USA
ASIA
Afghanistan, India, Israel, Japan, Malaysia
AUSTRALIA
New Zealand
AFRICA
Egypt, Botswana

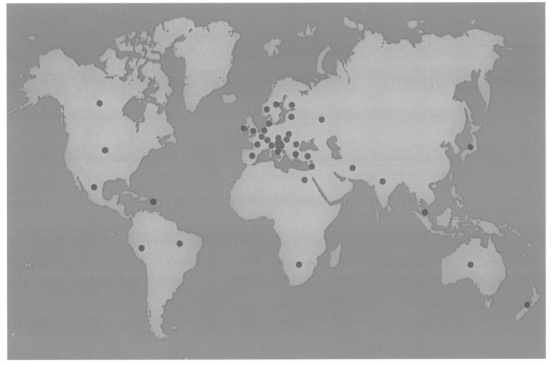

THOUSANDS OF
CROP CIRCLES
IN OVER FORTY
COUNTRIES

This village (population: 3,000) is renowned for its beautiful cottages and exquisite plants. The area is also famous for its barrows. It lies in the Test Valley, fifteen miles north of Winchester and five miles south of Andover. Stonehenge is approximately twenty miles away. The nearby Markway, one of Europe's oldest streets, was probably the road to Stonehenge in prehistoric times.

THE VILLAGE OF CHILBOLTON IN WEST HAMPSHIRE

Like many other British villages, Chilbolton (known as "Ceobaldinctura" in Saxon days) has ancient roots; in fact, Stone Age artifacts from this community can be seen in both the British Museum and the nearby Winchester Museum. Just recently, remnants of Roman settlements were found near the present telescope.

The land around the observatory belongs to the Leckford Estate of the John Lewis Group. Ben Gibbons, the manager of the estate, does not appreciate unexpected visitors.

A 360° panorama of Chilbolton from the telescope dish

This is the world's most advanced meteorological radar-station, located at 51°08' N and 01°26' W. It uses an adjustable 23-yard parabolic antenna and a 3-gigahertz Doppler polarization weather radar transmitter with a transmission radius of more than 124 miles. Along with two other radar transmitters on the frequency bands of 35 and 94 GHz, the observatory also has various experimental microwave communication systems, as well as various satellite receivers. National and international research on the university level is carried out regularly here. The Chilbolton Radio Communications Research Unit, constructed in 1965, is owned by the British government as part of the Rutherford Appleton Laboratory, which in turn is part of the Central Laboratory of the Research Council (CLRC).

The observatory serves mainly meteorological research.

It is interesting to note that the edge of the "passport photo" is directed toward the personnel office and the "technical message" lies exactly in the direction of the telescope.

It is 7:00 a.m., Tuesday morning, August 14, in the first year of the new millennium. An employee of the Chilbolton Observatory notices a strangely patterned, somewhat rectangular patch in the wheat field outside his office. Other employees notice it too, because it was not there the day before. But the wheat is too high, so no clear design is recognizable from the flat angle, not even from the telescope dish. No one gives it another thought.

A few days later a woman rides by on her horse. With the eyes of an expert, she spots the sharp lines in the wave of wheat plants and suspects another crop circle. After her ride, she emails her photographer friend, Lucy Pringle, who knows from experience that speed is necessary to keep angry farmers from immediately mowing the damaged fields.

On Monday, August 20, Lucy begins to investigate the terrain with her equipment. She flies over the field several times with the little flying apparatus she rents for that task and is astounded at what she sees!

2001—
CONTACT!

Photographs of the "Code Strip," taken with high tripods, indicate 136 standing cylinders laid out like a giant crossword puzzle.

She discovers two formations: 1) a long strip, perhaps a kind of computer chip or some type of symbol never seen before. It looks like a modern carpet or a housing settlement made of children's blocks. 2) a smaller, squarer formation less than 91 yards from the first, not quickly recognizable from the air. These are no longer crop circles, they are the first crop *rectangles* — a new trend in the sign-language of crop fields!

Later that day, her enthusiasm dampened by exhaustion, Lucy develops and studies her new photographs. Holding the prints at a certain angle and unfocusing her eyes a bit, she is shocked to discover — staring right back at her — *a face.*

She scans a few pictures immediately and sends them by email to computer expert Paul Vigay, asking him for help with the "computer-chip-formation," which she cannot understand. He calls back within minutes, for he has instantly recognized the resemblance to the SETI-message from Arecibo!

Vigay realizes that this formation had been conceived as a message in a universal binary code to communicate with some possible extraterrestrial species. The similarities are immediately obvious. He also recognizes fine differences to SETI's message.

If these formations are authentic, Lucy thought, then the world needs to know about them! Within two hours, she put the best images on her Web site. At the same time, she informed several friends who were circle-experts. At once they began to investigate on their own: Can these images be authentic? How could such a face be counterfeited? They sent the photos to associates, so that the pictures were soon being examined by a group of well-known alternative scientists.

Video stills of "The Face"

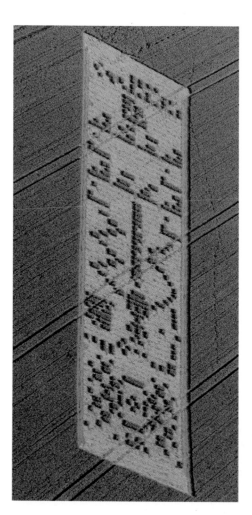

Lucy then called the head of the Chilbolton Observatory, Darcy Ladd. "If you want to see what fantastic crop-art is lying in the field outside your windows, then take a look at my Web site!" she told her. In fact, the telescope crew first saw the alien face not outside their building, but on Lucy's site. Ladd assured her that nothing unusual had turned up on their radar screens on the days before the appearance of the formations. Her employees had told her that the first imprint had still stood alone on the field on Saturday, so that the second one must have been added on Sunday or early Monday morning. Unfortunately the video surveillance of the observatory does not extend into the grain fields.

The story spread like wildfire. All the professional crop circle experts between Dorset and Wessex turned up almost immediately, some taking more spectacular video, films, and photographs from the air. Various private investigations were made and the usual measurements were taken: The ET-photo covers 145 by 165 feet including its "frame," and the long "pixel code" formation is nearly 90 by 265 feet (painstakingly measured by Charles R. Mallett).

Later Lucy brought a TV crew to film the scene. She buried several 25-milliliter bottles of water inside and outside the formation, as she has done before with other signs, to test later for energy levels. She was also able to establish that within both formations, the stalks had not been broken, but only bent at their bases. The conclusion was unavoidable: In the "written" history of man, an extraterrestrial intelligence has never so clearly and tangibly spoken and revealed himself to us!

Report from Charles R. Mallett, an experienced circles researcher and photographer, on visiting the Chilbolton Formations

The Face and the Answer

Late Wednesday evening (8/22/01), I received a phone call from Mark Fussell, editor of the Crop Circle Connector Web site, informing me of two new crop glyphs next to the radio telescope near Chilbolton in Hampshire. Mark's normally calm, composed demeanor was unmistakably emotional. He was in fact, hysterical.

"What is it? What is it?" I asked anxiously.

"Switch on your computer and see for yourself, you won't believe this one, it's truly amazing!" he spoke with a trill.

So I switched on my antiquated computer and waited impatiently for it to power up. Gradually the images appeared on my screen. I gasped in total amazement and disbelief. Could that haunting face actually be in a field of wheat or was this a computer-generated scam? A couple of quick phone calls confirmed that the face and its bizarre attendant glyph were indeed there in the field. Suddenly, I felt that the whole crop circle phenomenon had taken a quantum leap forward and a new episode in the history of crop circles had begun. My excitement, like Mark's, was palpable.

I made the decision there and then to go the very next day to the radio telescope in Hampshire, some forty miles from our home in Wiltshire. It was a workday, but I excused myself from it, headed for Hampshire with my partner, and arrived on the scene late morning. The weather conditions were dismal with steady rain falling, as it had been throughout the previous night and into the morning. Disregarding the adverse weather conditions, our hearts were racing as we approached the first of the two formations: the Face.

The Face

From an aerial perspective this was a truly remarkable crop glyph, one that we considered so staggering, we could barely accept that it was in a crop field at all. But it was in a crop field and we were to be some of the first people to walk within it. We wound a course through the network of woven paths consisting of hundreds of standing "cylinders" of varying size, each one individually and skillfully carved out of the ripe wheat.

As we stepped into the Face, the first thing we noticed was the total absence of mud and broken stems within the formation, either on or between the laid and woven crop. This was in unmistakable contrast to the large and obvious muddy boot prints we were leaving on all parts of the formation we explored.

Although these formations had been there for some considerable time, it appeared that hardly anyone had ventured into the field. This is not too surprising, considering that this area is well away from the usual circle hot-spots and is rarely visited by circle hunters or researchers. Apparently, somebody just got lucky whilst flying over the area and brought it to the attention of various researchers.

From the ground this was a totally incomprehensible image. As we wandered amid hundreds of standing cylinders, it became apparent that the style of the lay was as unique and interesting as the actual image created by the positioning of the cylinders. Between all of the standing cylinders, the laid crop had been whipped around into undulations of wheat, with each wave folding and overlapping the other. From zero elevation it seemed quite irregular and incoherent. However, when we referred to the aerial view, it was apparent that the elaborate floor construction was a critical factor in achieving the overall effect.

This entirely new method of construction uses a familiar dot-matrix technique found in printing of tonal images (such as photographs) to create depth and definition. It is also found in needlepoint. At the very least, the glyph must be considered an artistic achievement of the highest magnitude; at best, it marks what could be considered a revolution in the history of crop circle execution and image representation. I believe this revolution in crop circles is consistent with the pace and the intensity of the shift in planetary consciousness.

In the opinion of this writer there is absolutely no way that this formation could have been created by humans. In fact, the methodology used in the creation of the formation is so far beyond the capabilities of known circle-fakers, it is ludicrous to discuss it further.

The Answer

The attendant crop glyph in the Chilbolton telescope field is an equally astounding event. This formation is heralded as the most decodable representation that has ever graced the crop fields of this magical land. While further research may reveal more data and insights, on the surface it seems to be a direct reply to a binary code message beamed into space by NASA in November 1974 (targeting star cluster M13). It may well be a response. Why not? In my opinion, everything about the formation suggests that it is a genuine and totally anomalous happening. From the air this glyph appears to be laid out on a massive stone or brick-type slab. It also has the familiar visual effect of a cross-stitched tapestry. As with the face, the agent employed an elaborate artistic method of crop flattening to achieve a very specific aerial effect.

On the ground, all the individual standing sections were finished to a very high standard. Everything was extremely neat, with sharp cut edges throughout the entire formation. As with the Face, the floor construction was intriguing and well executed. What can clearly be perceived from the air is not at all apparent on the ground.

After walking in the laid areas for some time, it became evident how this effect was systematically created with the end result in "mind." First, the border (or frame) went down, as it did with the Face. Then large wads of crop "fell" down on a pre-arrangement of short slender paths that crisscross the bulk of the laid area, creating a brick effect. Once again, we are looking at an entirely new construction style for the crop circle phenomenon.

It is tempting to speculate from these examples that the twenty-year learning curve is coming to an end and communications are about to become more overt. Perhaps this formation and its attendant Face foreshadow a series of direct contacts?

What can be said for certain, is that these two formations represent a departure from the norm. For anyone who is sufficiently open, I believe these examples clearly articulate that we are not alone, and that direct communication with an agency capable of far more than three-dimensional hoaxes is most certainly happening.

The level of interest generated by recent crop circle events is now unprecedented. Media interest has been so intense of late that one is almost expecting a major debunking scam to occur at any moment. Thus far, there is no sign of a destructive extravaganza characteristic of the Doug and Dave fabrication.

Ordinary people are experiencing shifts in their personal paradigms as a result of seeing these images on their TV and computer screens or in the print media. Many are affected by this and concomitant events. Like the hundredth monkey phenomenon, it is only a matter of time before the consciousness of the larger general public will be affected at a deep level. This progress could, of course, be interrupted by government authorities should they decide to clamp down once again on the free flow of information. No doubt they will try, sooner or later.

In the year before this sensational discovery, some of the crop detectives believed that there had been hints of more sophisticated pixel-matrices and moirés in other crop circles.

Were these artworks perhaps just practice sessions or trial runs of anonymous artists, training for their newest masterworks? Had the artists been perfecting their techniques? If we view the progression of this agrarian pointillism more closely, such a conclusion is almost inevitable.

EXTRATERRESTRIAL MATRICES

The "Electromagnetic Field" of Avebury Trusloe was seen in 2000.

The "Carpet" of All Cannings in 2001 shows positive and negative dots within one formation for the first time.

The weaving art of the aliens, shown at the intricately woven grid of East Kennet in 2000, consists of 1600 rectangles of varying sizes from dark to bright within a 200-foot circle.

The "Pillow" of Windmill Hill showed a sort of grid-induced 3D effect.

The circled square of Etchilhampton 1997 had 780 single rectangles.

From simple checkersboards to matrix-photographs. What a quantum leap in the evolution of crop circles!

Lucy Pringle told me that she found the shading of the face especially phenomenal. The stalks around each of the small bushel-dots all seem to be individually bent, laid, and woven. Also, it is remarkable that the newer Chilbolton formations are the very first in which the content and the expressiveness stem primarily from the "positive" relief, i.e., of the plants still standing and not bent. This is a likely reason why the artists framed their work on this occasion for the very first time. But this is not the only reason the artists framed their work, as we will see later.

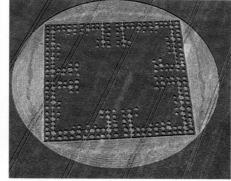

A squared circle with dots was the grid at Windmill Hill in 1999.

The 412 individual bushel matrix-dots of the face

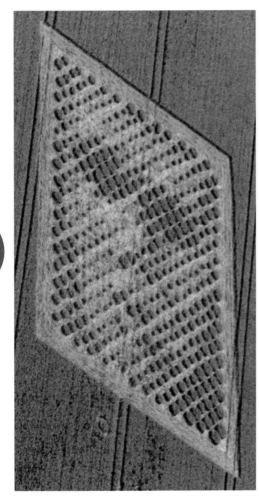

Standing in the middle of the field, one cannot recognize the subject.

The largest passport photo in the world is a bit "coarse-grained."

Note the immense difference in scale between the man and the photogram.

AUGUST 14, 2001
THE DAY ET
APPEARED

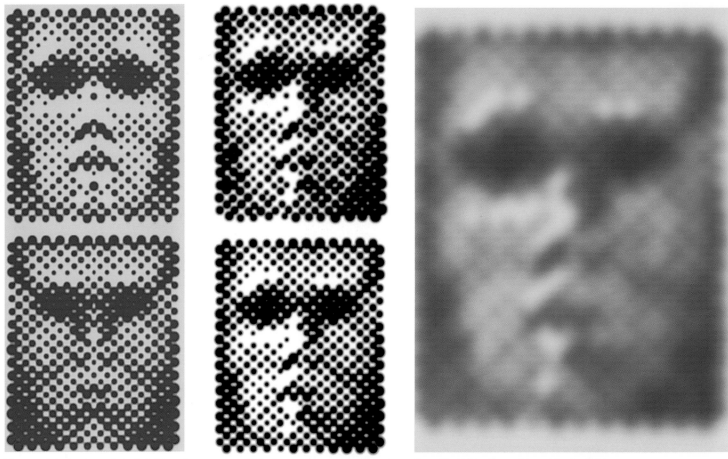

42

Mirrored duplication of the left (above) and right (below) sides of the face

(above) The face points as they have been found individually positioned in the field
(below) The idealized version by centering each point in the appropriate grid field

Report from Francine Blake on photographing and visiting Chilbolton Formations

Ms. Blake is founder/coordinator of the Wiltshire Crop Circle Study Group and editor of Spiral Magazine.

Last August I flew over the formations with two other members of the Wiltshire Crop Circle Study Group to photograph them. I usually take two cameras with me to photograph crop circles: a manual medium format Hasselblad (bought because the previous camera got totally ruined from exposure to crop circle energy, and I was told Hasselblad is the only camera that would sustain repeated exposure to radiation), and a digital one. We started to go around the formations and I took many shots with the manual camera and everything was fine. Next I started to use the digital one, which is usually a quicker process.

I took landscape pictures of the two formations and of the scroll with no problem, but whenever I tried to take an overhead picture of the face, the digital camera would go quite wild with warning lights, beeps, and the message that the film card was pushed out repeatedly flashing onto the screen (the card was not out of position). I persisted but whenever I was positioned directly over the face I experienced the same difficulties. Eventually I found an angle where the camera didn't react and got a good shot.

Back home I proceeded to download the card into my computer. I have two computers, a six-year old Mac and a two-year old G3 laptop. Both are equipped to take smart cards. As the laptop was a new addition and I was not too familiar with it, I thought I would download the images in the older computer. I have never had any problem doing this. As soon as the card was inserted the computer crashed. I switched it off and restarted it; it made awful grating noises and refused to come back to life. I tried the laptop. It also crashed, but upon restarting my Norton Utility program kicked in to repair whatever damage. I tried again and the same thing happened. This time I left it. The laptop seemed to be all right, but the dates changed to some time in the future, (maybe it's significant, who knows with crop circles!) and subsequently the mother-board cracked and had to be replaced. Crop circles are a costly business.

I called a computer expert to come fix my old Mac. After examining it at length, he told me all its memory had been used up!! I told him it happened when I tried to download the face (which I showed him). He looked startled and didn't believe me. The computer is still out of action. I am quite convinced the face is built on a complex grid that confuses our technology, maybe a hologram of some sort. I am also sending you the aerial photograph I took that day with the manual camera.

Afterwards we went in the formations. Chilbolton Observatory has restricted entry signs around its fences. It is quite forbidding; we went in anyway (the field is outside the periphery but right next to it) — all the while trying to look as invisible as possible as we spent some time measuring and photographing. The face is quite impossible to decipher at ground level and almost as large as a football pitch. The crop was of poor quality with the stems stunted (barely two feet tall), dry, brittle, and with little lustre, not too healthy looking. The overall impression at ground level was of chaos. The standing tufts that make the pixels were of many different sizes, some only a few stems wide (three or four stems), and the beautiful "flow" of the crop usually associated with crop circles was not there due to the complex pixilated nature of the design. In spite of all that, the plants did not look damaged to me, just dry. The extraordinary complexity of the lay, going this way and that without rhyme or reason, or so it seemed at ground level, precludes the possibility of doing it by "hand" with planks or rollers. Besides, the malfunctioning of the camera over the face is always a sure sign of a powerful energy field. I studied photography at Art School in the 60s and have done photography ever since. I have never experienced camera malfunctions anywhere else than in and around crop circles.

We laid down on the face's third eye for about an hour. That was quite an experience. The energy was very strong, I know some people who got quite close to the face formation but could not get in and turned back even after having driven several hours to get there. Seeing these two amazing messages so close to the Radio Telescope Observatory where people are glued to their computers' screen was really comical.

After visiting the face, we followed the tractor line that connects it to the script; we had an aerial photograph in hand so we could see the way to get into it. Without the photo we would not have been able to find it so easily, as the script was not visible from the face. It looked much neater than the face and the lay was tidy. We could see that the standing crops made precise designs but we could not imagine what they were as the scale was too big. The main impression we had was one of amazement that such large formations as those two, so close to the Observatory, should have made so little impact on the people working there. We surmised they were too busy looking at their computer screens to bother to look behind them. Standing in the formation watching the large dish scanning the heavens seemed to sum up the majority of human beings' attitudes towards new knowledge: They are unable to see it, let alone accept the immensity of such an occurrence!

Lucy Pringle did not have to wait long to have her pictures published. The British newspaper *Daily Mail* was the first to report the phenomenon. A few days later, the *Daily Express* followed. But that was all.

Of course, this was not the first time the press mishandled a crop circle story. The *Daily Mail* is well known for being aggressively negative toward crop-circle phenomena. Years ago its editors hired crop field counterfeiters to produce fake formations, ostensibly to prove how easy it is to do so. Whatever their motives, the British press has long had a negative attitude toward the phenomenon.

Besides, the rest of the press had already reported the previous week on the famous "Milk Hill" formation, so there was little interest in any new crop art.

But this "Six-Armed Julia Set" (see page 12) could not be ignored for "her" size alone. 409 circles covering a space of almost 100,000 square yards is truly astounding! This galactic formation must have been constructed during the previous night in pouring rain. And it was simply inconceivable that this task could have been done without leaving any traces. For this reason, many TV networks — from BBC to CNN, and Japanese and Australian channels — carried news about this formation.

The amount of activity in the fields during this period was considerable. Two days after Milk Hill and simultaneously with The Face, a formation was found near Huish (see next page) which by some is interpreted as the representation of a radio broadcast. This octagonal formation appears authentic because of its light circular lines alone, as you cannot walk through the crop without destroying its clear-cut design. The authenticity is further supported by the discovery of unusual extended stalk knots.

The report on page 27 of the *Daily Mail* edition of August 28, 2001. At first glance the article appears to be serious, but on a closer look it is superficial and mean-spirited. Besides connecting the Chilbolton event to a report on a new *Star Trek* series, the newspaper suggests that if the image is not counterfeit, it must just be an echo of the original SETI message.

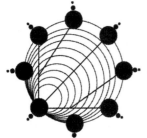

This "broadcasting" sign was found in the neighboring county on the same day as "The Face."

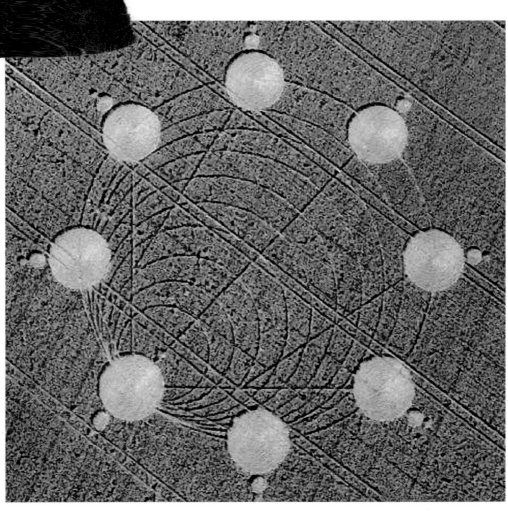

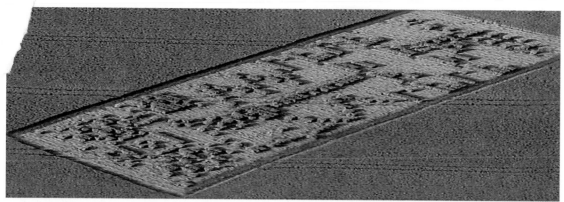

August 19, 2001. E.T. has replied!

The crop circle response of ET intelligence

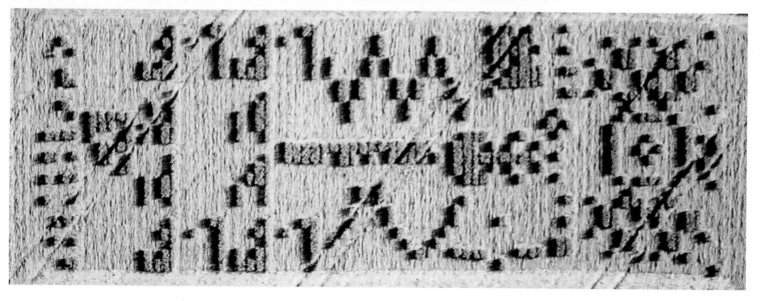

There had been preliminary signs in the area of Chilbolton in the early 1990s: On May 25, 1992, a "Ringed Circle with Arrow" appeared. Its discovery was connected to the sighting of a "Star of David" UFO. Though the sighting was denied by officials, they would not explain why more than a dozen Lynx army helicopters flew over the observatory at that time. Two months later, on July 30, 1994, "double-ringed quarter-arc segments" appeared, and on July 1 of that same year, "two equal-sized circles" were seen.

Looking back now, it's surprisingly obvious how the messages had been carefully and gradually prepared by the ETs. The senders of the crop-faxes were preparing us cleverly but gently two years before. Even the cornfield in front of the Chilbolton Observatory had already received a matrix imprint in June of 1999 — a rare dot-matrix formation was beamed into the young barley crop. Being government land (closed to the public), this event has been kept a secret; only a few rather unclear photos exist.

Did the authors want to tell us, "Yes, we know you have recognized that fractal structures can be used to amplify signals! We also use fractal structures to broadcast! Occupy yourselves even more with this fundamental geometry and mathematics!"

RESPONSE:
PHASE I

A simple double-circle, 60 feet in diameter, appeared near Chilbolton in 1992.

The first crop formation near the observatory, measuring 115 by 66 yards, is one of the larger "medium-sized" signs. Each of the 146 dots measures almost 3 yards in diameter.

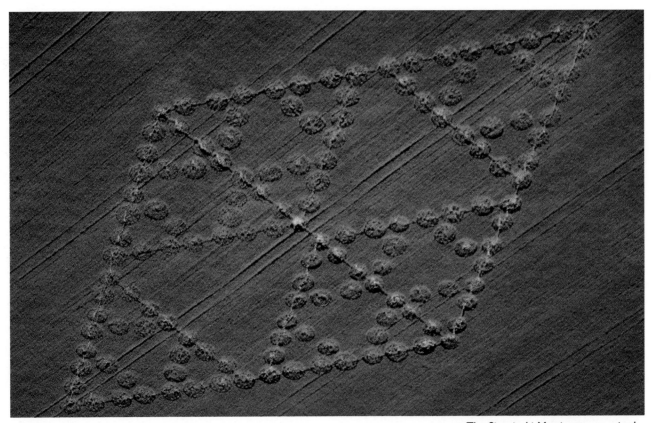

The Sierpinski Matrix was seen in the
Chilbolton Observatory field on June 12, 1999.

The huge "diamond" within the young barley crop indicates a vital structure for the future. In this apparently rather simple scheme, there is such enormous potential! As we will see later, this structure is part of a crucial geometrical function which the circlemakers are hinting to us with a hidden mathematical message.

ET seems to have thought: "There is too much jungle around the Arecibo Observatory, so we cannot send our answer there. We'll just do it here in the wheat field next to this observatory!"

In any case, no one was thinking about such connections at that time. Only in retrospect is the gradual, "soft" development of the grain-mailings of Chilbolton clearly apparent.

Another connection has developed by understanding the importance of non-Euclidean fractal geometry. The first fractal formations appeared in the mid-90s; in the meantime, there have been dozens of them. This geometry is discussed further on page 104.

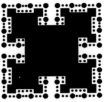

The Butterfly-Fractal of August 13-14, 2000, in the Chilbolton Observatory field.

Butterfly ground shots

In the summer of 2000, there were an especially great number of complex diagrams. The most fascinating (first spotted exactly one year before the ET portrait of 2001) was the "Butterfly Fractal." It measured approximately 50 x 90 square yards and was suddenly visible to the telescope crew in the opposite field from where the "Antenna Fractal" had been discovered. Was the message meant for them?

This relief, composed of both flattened and unchanged grain, began a new era of artistic virtuosity. Its subject matter aroused a lot of controversy, too. Was this fractal supposed to represent two brain hemispheres, or a hint at telepathy, or a sun symbol? Not knowing which, how should it be named? Finally, "Butterfly" became widely accepted.

This perfect fractal formation was constructed of 149 circles and rings of many sizes. A year later, the same ring formation was repeated in pixel form at Chilbolton, with the obvious purpose of establishing some sort of connection.

The tractor track occurs at an almost exact right angle to the telescope dish — with a seemingly intended 9° deflection.

Just as in the "Sierpinski Diamond Formation" of 1999, the changes in the field were hardly visible from the flat ground immediately outside. At first there were also no footpaths from outside to the diagram. Placed at almost exactly a right angle to the telescope, the diagram was apparently meant to refer to some aspect of sending and receiving — a hypothesis that was to be confirmed a year later!

The computer reconstruction at right demonstrates the extremely complicated 24 steps needed to construct only half of this diagram. Such a formation could never be simply stamped onto a grain-field by people, in a few hours at night, without leaving any traces behind.

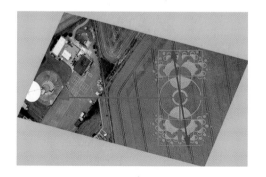

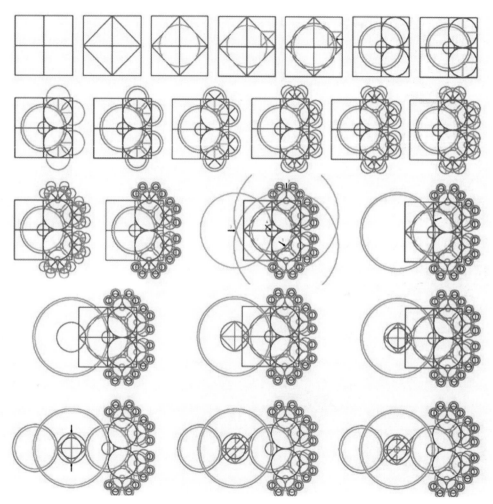

The custom in the civilized world, according to universal standards of etiquette, is to introduce oneself politely to a stranger. In lieu of a business card and a personal handshake, ET had the ingenious idea of simply beaming us his portrait.

Why haven't the aliens introduced themselves in person, or at least by means of telepathy or via the long-awaited radio signals to SETI?

Let's assume that such direct contacts have happened numerous times through the years. Perhaps these contacts have been suppressed by world leaders or organizations unsympathetic to such news!

Special computer software accentuation of the three-dimensional quality of the grain portrait demonstrates that the expression on the face changes slightly according to the angle of the sun's rays, showing a "morning," "noon," and "evening" face.

AUGUST 2001:
RESPONSE - PHASE III-I

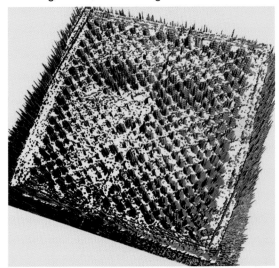

My own hypothesis is that ET chose this surprising — and less shocking — way of making contact in order to circumvent the intentions of those would-be world controllers. Of course these "leaders" are still trying to blame some kind of crazy freaks for the crop designs, and most of the mass media are playing along, either out of stupidity or in overanxious subservience. But the more facts we discover, the less credible the claims of the ignorers. These facts can be found in the details.

The Chilbolton agriglyphs can be seen as the definitive turning point. What was previously just a hypothesis can no longer be denied: We are not the only ones in the universe! The greatest adventure of mankind has begun!

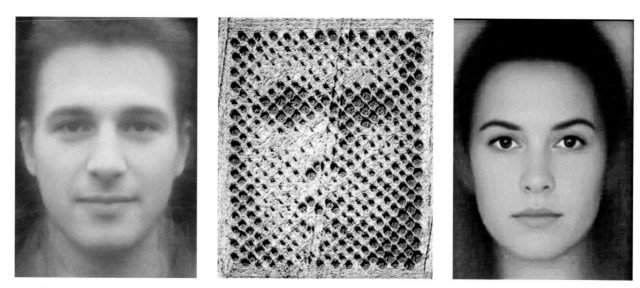

The average proportions of human faces and those of the alien head are not the same: The ET skull is longer and larger.

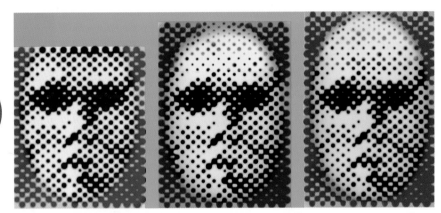

By completing the alien face with the missing part, a very different appearance is evident.

A matrix-point measures about three yards.

60

Was Mars a populated planet long ago? Did the survivors of a Martian catastrophe journey to Earth and establish an advanced civilization long before the beginning of recorded history? Are we related to the Ancient Martians as the Chilbolton message seems to say?

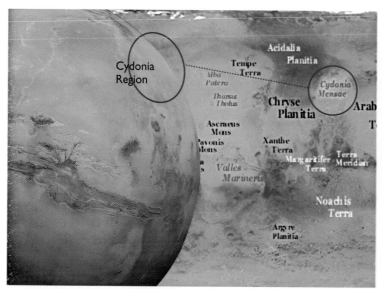

Mars Surface Projection

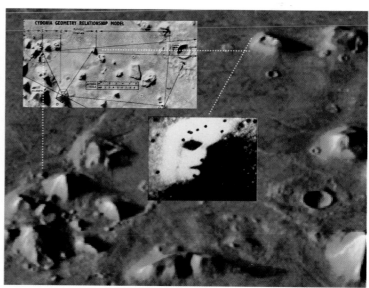

Mars Cydonia Region

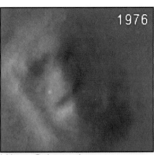

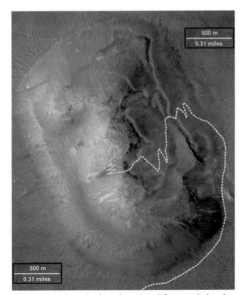

The formation, exaggerated in a
three-dimensional computer simulation

In 1976 the Viking spaceship took 300,000 pictures of our neighboring planet. Four years later, NASA's Vincent Di Pietro discovered in photo 35A72 "the raised picture of a humanoid face." He calculated a respectable length of 9 miles for this "greatest artistic sculpture ever." After further analysis, he was sure — despite the imminent ridicule of experts and the press — that this had to be a symmetrical sculptural monument made by intelligent beings. Further photos show the same face from other perspectives at different times of the day. And only 9.5 miles from this Mars face: a destroyed city of huge pyramids.

There was an attempt to discredit this view by means of newer, sharper NASA photos from another perspective. Nevertheless, the characteristics of a head are still visible despite many thousands of years of obvious erosion. What kind of Martian civilization has left its tracks here?

1976

Viking Orbiter photo

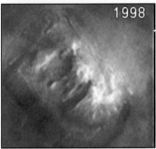

1998

Global Surveyor photo

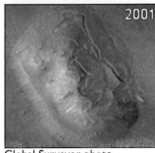

2001

Global Surveyor photo

A previously calculated optimal footpath leads
to the nose of the 300-yard high stone face.

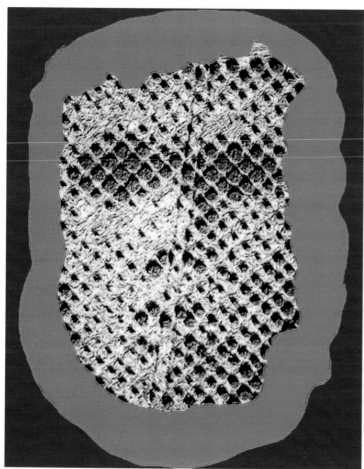

The Crop Face of Chilbolton

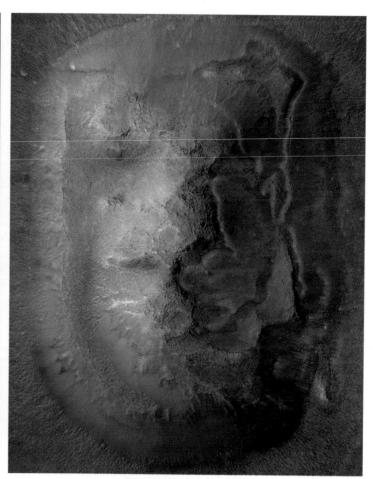

The Rock Face of Cydonia

63

Comparison of the Mars rock face and the Chilbolton wheat-field face demonstrates the same harmonious face matrix.

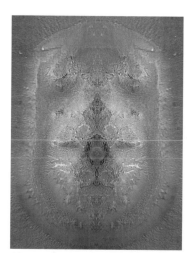 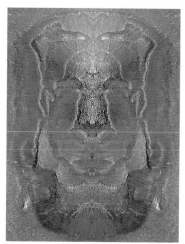

Mirroring of the eroded left and right sides of the Mars Face

Recognizing the Mars Face is essential when you study the Chilbolton head. Considering the similarity of the proportions and the strange tractor traces as a reference to the shading on the Martian rock face, the evidence is even more striking: There must be a connection!

Considering Pyramid City (9.5 miles from the face) with its tetrahedral layout, there are several more striking similarities between the Mars Face and Chilbolton: Besides the layout of the different buildings (i.e., their ruins), according to the sacred geometry, there is also a group of four rocks at the center of the City — arranged in a square from whose center the Mars Face lies exactly in the direction of the Mars summer solstice, approximately 500,000 years ago!

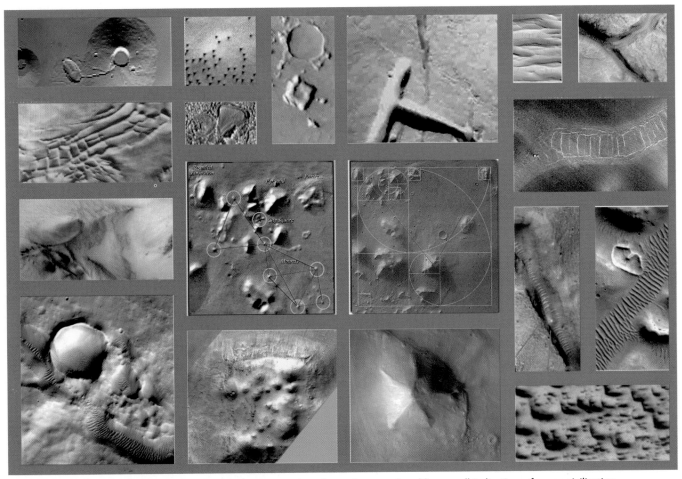

In the meantime, a number of unusual structures have been discovered on Mars — all indicating a former civilization.

THE COSMIC CORRESPONDENCE:

August 19, 2001: Response-Phase III-2:
A more than unusual date — already at the beginning of the new milennium there was a taste of the fulfillment of our galactic longings.

A civilization which has sped ahead of us would like to offer us a hand. Is there any possible first step more tactful than just leaving a message in nature? Now it is up to us to take advantage of this unique opportunity.

A close look at the interplanetary dialog reveals ten basic differences — some very subtle, a few more definitive — between the initial message sent into space and ET's reply.

In the upper half of the message there are some essential distinctions: from the added number among the constitutive biological elements — suggesting a different DNA-structure —to the greater number of nucleotides of the three-fold curved alien DNA.

At first, one is struck by the alien's rather different appearance from us. The pixels at the side tell us that there are at least twice as many ETs as humans, but they are only half as large.

The location of ET's civilization is defined in a somewhat strange manner. There is room for interpretation, but I feel that wherever they are, there is also their huge crop-sign beam-apparatus with which they transmit all their crop-circle communications.

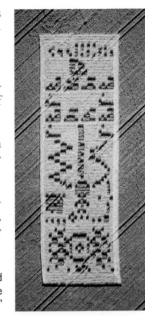

In the exact bird's-eye view of the digitally processed aerial photo, there is an interesting distortion of the "grain papyrus-roll."

DETAILS OF THE RESPONSE: TEN BASIC DIFFERENCES

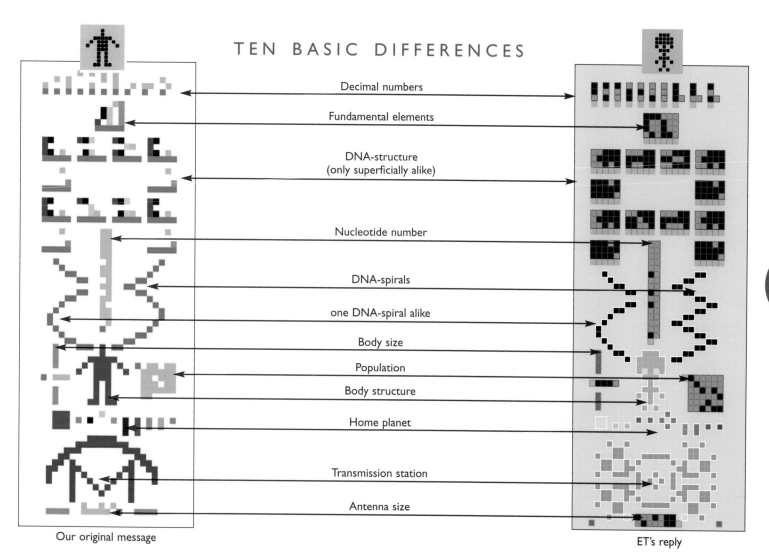

TEN BASIC DIFFERENCES

Decimal numbers

Fundamental elements

DNA-structure
(only superficially alike)

Nucleotide number

DNA-spirals

one DNA-spiral alike

Body size

Population

Body structure

Home planet

Transmission station

Antenna size

Our original message

ET's reply

69

Decimal numbers 1-10
Here there is no difference between our message and the alien answer,
so decimal calculation must be known to them.

In the second message row there is this intriguing and important difference: While our message stated only five basic life-giving elements on Earth, the ETs mention silicon as a further essential element. That does not mean that their life is built on silicon, but that their form of life is similar to ours with the addition of the element silicon.

The newest research says, however, that we also cannot do without silicon in our biological structure. That could mean that the aliens only want to correct our message. But other rows of the message contradict this thought: Supposing that the element silicon is life-essential for our cosmic friends, and their body chemistry otherwise agrees with ours, then this factor may have something to do with their further evolutionary development.

ET DIFFERENCE # 1: SIX FUNDAMENTAL ELEMENTS

70

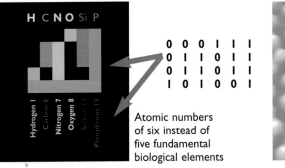

Atomic numbers
of six instead of
five fundamental
biological elements

Silicon surface
in raster-tunnel
microscope

The six important elements constitute 97% of our human body mass: 65% oxygen as part of water and most organic molecules (also molecular oxygen), 18% carbon (the backbone of all organic molecules), 10% hydrogen as part of all organic molecules and of water, 3% as component of proteins and nucleic acids, 1% phosphorus as part of cell membranes and of energy storage molecules (also a constituent of bone). In the human body there are usually only 5 to 10 grams of silicon, most likely acquired from the environment. There is dissolved silicic acid in drinking water and silicate dust in the air we breathe. Silicon plays a key, but not fully understood, role in the growth of hair, nails, and bones. Interestingly, at the site of a bone fracture, silicon content increases 50-fold in the collagen web. Although natural silicon-carbon bonds are extremely rare on Earth, they can be created synthetically.

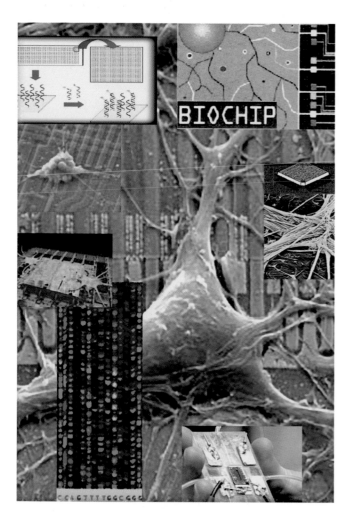

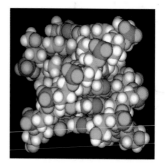

The present biotechnological developments on our planet have only made vague steps toward interaction between living cells and electronic circuits. How far has ET advanced in bio-engineering and the symbiosis of high-tech and bionics?

The idea of silicon-based bio-computers integrated into the mind-body continuum is not unlikely. While we humans still have to get our regular medical check-ups, the alien species has perhaps already eliminated this chore by inner error-detectors and self-activating, attached repair programs — much like we know in the computer world.

Also, controlling computers with neural signals — as the navigation control panels of the crashed Roswell UFO indicate — might be an output of that genetic mutation.

Thanks to silicon integration, what we consider science fiction is routine in ET's world!

Based on the additional silicon element, ET's DNA structure, as relayed through the grain-fax, seems to be somewhat unusual — although the pixel matrix shows no visible distinction. Due to the different decoding key based on Difference #1, however, there seems to be a surprising new gene-structure: Silicon replaces phosphorus in position 5, as the decoding modus is determined by the order of the fundamental chemical elements.

ET DIFFERENCE # 2: DIFFERENT DNA STRUCTURE

Because of the change in the code, all phosphorus molecules (PO4) are obviously replaced in ET's DNA by silicon-oxygen-4-tetrahedrons.

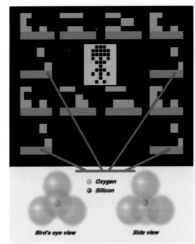

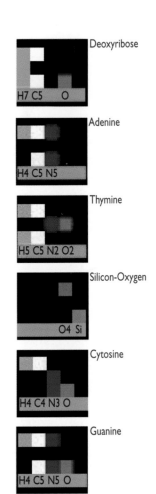

Deoxyribose
H7 C5 O

Adenine
H4 C5 N5

Thymine
H5 C5 N2 O2

Silicon-Oxygen
O4 Si

Cytosine
H4 C4 N3 O

Guanine
H4 C5 N5 O

Binary representation of the amino-acids

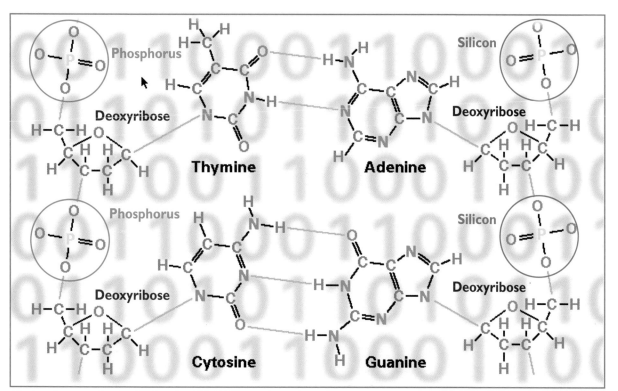

Phosphorus

Silicon

Deoxyribose

Thymine

Adenine

Deoxyribose

Phosphorus

Silicon

Deoxyribose

Cytosine

Guanine

Deoxyribose

All phosphorus molecules PO4 within ET's DNA are changed to silicon-oxygen-molecules SiO4.

Arbitrary sequence part of the DNA-ladder

73

ET DIFFERENCE # 3: THE NUCLEOTIDE NUMBERS

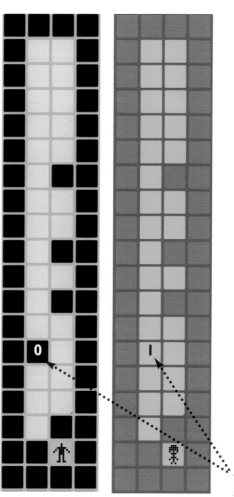

Judged on the basis of ET's entire answer, the aliens are some steps ahead of us in their evolution — if one sees the ability for genetic manipulation as progress!

If we consider the minute modifications of our original Arecibo message in detail, we can conclude that their mental abilities are on a superior level. The formula for ET's molecular structure is, as we have seen, almost identical to that of humans. But from their answer we can determine that they have a very exact knowledge of our Earthly DNA structure, or at least a better knowledge than the scientists of the Human Genome Project do!

In 1974, Carl Sagan estimated the number of our nucleotides, i.e., the base pairs of a single DNA-strand, at approximately 4 billion. Having to name a concrete 32-bit binary number, he estimated it at 4,294,441,822. But the alien message establishes their ET-DNA-spiral at exactly 4,294,966,110 sequences.

That is about a half a million more than we believed in those days. The Human Genome Project, however, accepts momentarily "only" 3.5 billion nucleotides for homo sapiens!

This one pixel makes the difference: 524,288 DNA base pairs.

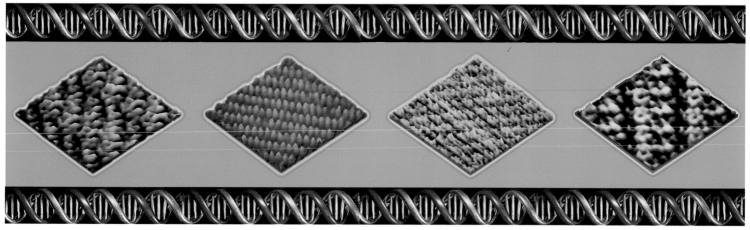

Adenine, Guanine, Thymine, and Cytosine enlarged to atomic scale

In the binary nucleotide number of our message to the ETs (and also in the then-stated number of the Earth's population), there were a few irrelevant zeroes added in the lower digits to show the alien decoders that these were mathematical and not graphic messages.

The DNA section of the individual amino acids described by the aliens in data-packets #2 and #3 is enough for us to be able to describe the whole DNA-strand. The repetition of the molecules, together with the nucleotide number, allows one to deduce the whole structure of the helix. Besides, an analysis of the chemical structures would show that only the bases adenine and thymine, as well as the bases cytosine and guanine, can directly connect with each other.

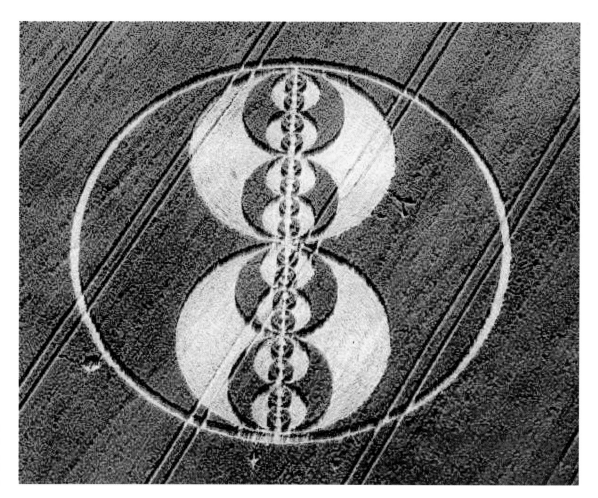

This 2001 crop circle near Stanton St. Bernard, Wiltshire, possibly depicts DNA.

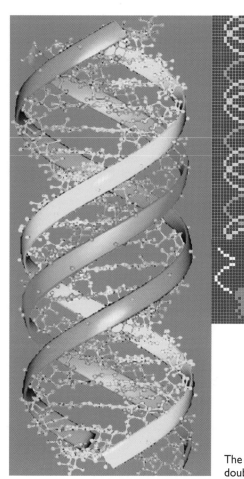

ET
DIFFERENCE
4:
MORE
DNA
SPIRALS

77

The evolutionary step from Earthly
double-helix to ET's triple-helix

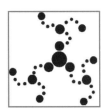

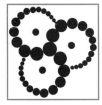

These earlier grain-pictures hinted at a triple-helix.

One of the most astounding ET messages is the indication there is a triple DNA with the integration of silicon. Although there are currently a few elementary optimizing experiments in our planet's scientific communities, no attempts at something of this scale have occurred — simply because we do not have the knowledge. To add a third strand to the double helix seems to be the logical consequence of the tetrahedral structure of the silicon-oxygen molecule. This may also have led to a third brain "hemisphere" in the alien head, which may give them highly evolved telepathic abilities.

From the alien message one may gain the impression that our cosmic friends are inclined to help us move in this direction. Why would they mention it if that were not the case? With a biological, mineralogical, and molecular ability of this quality, we may easily be able to solve many of our external and internal problems, such as medical (e.g., longevity), technical (e.g., antigravity), philosophical (e.g., grasping higher laws of life), sociological (e.g., better conflict-solving strategies) — all of which could enable us to live together in peace and freedom.

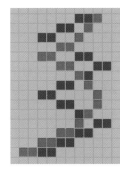

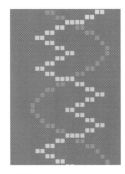

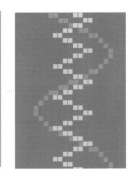

These two variations of triple-DNA are conceivable from their message.

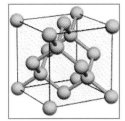

SILICON is a "jack of all trades" and a "genius" among the elements. Si is the basic medium for all areas of modern electronics where light is used for calculations. In crystal form it is found in every computer chip, for light can be freely manipulated in this element; thus it is able to connect unequal partners, e.g., as an intermediary between light and electronics.

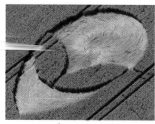

Here we find the first measurement in the messages. There is only one possibility for a unit of measurement: the wavelength in which we sent the message, exactly 12.6 cm (approximately 5 inches). That was transposed to the human average height of 176.4 cm (approximately 5 feet 9 inches). The figure received for the skinny alien man was a binary 8, which multiplies to 100.8 cm (3 1/3 feet)! So while they just reach to our navels, their greater brain volume implies that we cannot reach their IQ.

As phosphorus is substituted within the alien organism, the percentage of silicon within their body seems to be in the same weight dimension. That means, considering the small size of their bodies, they have implemented approximately half a pound of silicon into their body structure.

The ET body-logo hints also at larger eyes, similar to the message of the crop circle at Bishop Cannings, Wiltshire, on August 23, 1999 (see above photo). Their weight can only be estimated, perhaps at 55 pounds. But actual weight is only relevant in regards to the gravity on their home planet.

The "little green men" are really small, but not necessarily green.

Comparison of body sizes

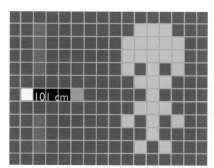

101 cm

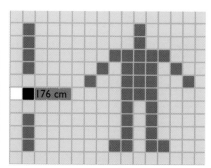

176 cm

The speed of light 29 979 245 800 cm per sec divided by the wavelength radio frequency of 2 380 000 000 per sec equals 12,596 cm (415 2/3 feet).

ET DIFFERENCE
7:
THE POPULATION

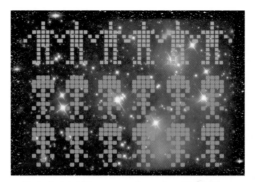

Today's 6.1 billion terranians plus 12.7 billion ETs equals approximately 19 billion known space inhabitants.

It is not very easy to decode the message relating the size of the ET population. Since the crop art has been disturbed by tractor tracks, blown by the wind, and distorted by shadows, it is not surprising that the resulting pictures have been the basis of a number of false estimates. Also, a certain amount of concentration is necessary to translate the 34-bit binary number. If you calculate correctly, the different digits add up to 12,742,213,502 aliens.

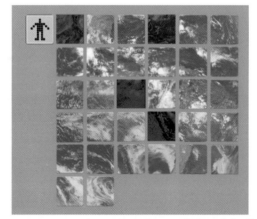

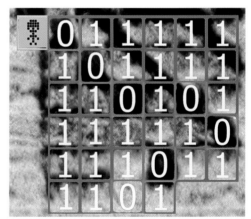

In contrast, the population of the Earth 27 years ago was 4,292,853,750.

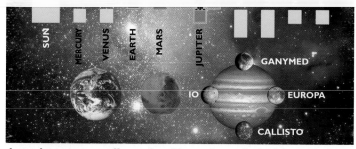

astounding. In contrast to our single planet, they mention three places.

The size of the alien solar system is somewhat smaller, e.g., the sun is made up of only four squares (or bits) instead of the nine in the human solar system. Saturn, Uranus, and Neptune are also drawn smaller, but I believe the ETs have made these depictions smaller to be able to show their alien beamer without distortion and make it easier for us to understand its function and the overall transmission.

What points to the fact that they originally lived on Earth is that they highlighted the Earth (although they are not here now), their features are similar to ours, and they understand and are interested in us. Indeed, some scientists have found evidence of a long ago alien presence in strange monuments (built with techniques unknown today) and sculptures of ancient cultures (e.g., the Nazca lines of Peru), (even biblical) mythological interpretations, and a lot of inexplicable archeological artifacts (e.g., Sumerian cylinder seals depicting celestial knowledge that cannot have existed at that time, mysterious cave paintings, crystal skulls, etc.).

What points to the fact that they lived on Mars is that they highlighted Mars (by elevating the bit for Mars although Mars is seemingly uninhabited now), that their features show a great resemblance to the Mars Face, that there are many artificial structures on Mars, and that — though there has been more water on Mars in times past — it is still there according to NASA's latest findings.

What points to the fact that they live today on the four biggest Jupiter moons is that they elevate Jupiter (as one square within four squares), place this square in the center of the beamer, and answered our message in such a short time. NASA itself says life is most probable within our solar system on Jupiter's Moon Europa, that these moons consist mainly of silicon, and that many crop-circle formations depict the Jupiter moons.

Naturally there are other interpretations of the home planet answer, but none of them seem as feasible. That ET lives in three places at once seems improbable, since they would have been noticed by us on Earth. And there also does not seem to be much happening now on Mars — in obvious contradiction to earlier times, if we judge from the artifacts left behind.

Still, it seems unlikely that another solar system has the same number of planets, is the same size, and has the same relative position as ours.

Just as we in our message placed an Earthman directly over the proper planet pixel — saying, in effect, that we live here — in the ET answer, the alien person is pictured over Mars, the logical point between all the three planets when drawn in a raised position. Additional evidence of life on the four Jupiter moons is supported by NASA's prediction of water and silicon there.

Surfaces of the moon Europa, favored by NASA for possible extraterrestrial life

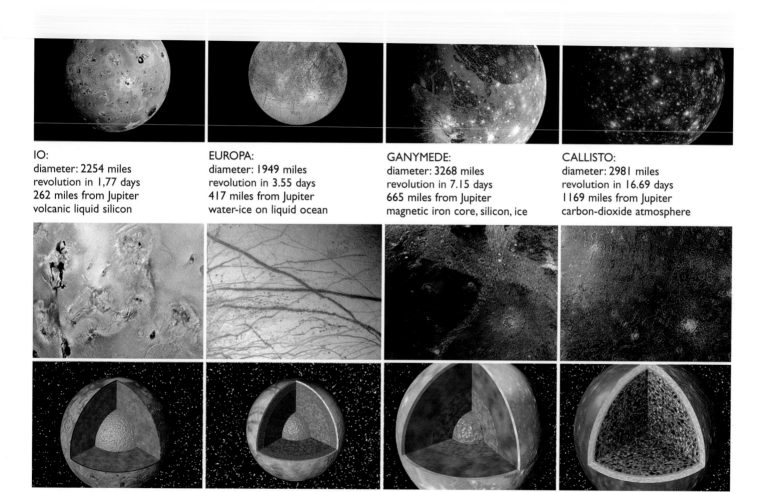

IO:
diameter: 2254 miles
revolution in 1,77 days
262 miles from Jupiter
volcanic liquid silicon

EUROPA:
diameter: 1949 miles
revolution in 3.55 days
417 miles from Jupiter
water-ice on liquid ocean

GANYMEDE:
diameter: 3268 miles
revolution in 7.15 days
665 miles from Jupiter
magnetic iron core, silicon, ice

CALLISTO:
diameter: 2981 miles
revolution in 16.69 days
1169 miles from Jupiter
carbon-dioxide atmosphere

Do these crop circles point to Jupiter's moons?

View of the Jupiter moons through a good telescope

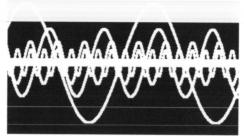

Movements of the four moon satellites around Jupiter (middle line)

ber of surprises. While Io is still quite active volcanically, sufficient conditions for lower life — as seen by our scientists — appear possible on the other moons.

But life may evolve in a completely different way under different ecological conditions to withstand much higher or lower temperatures, to develop a totally different energy transfer system, or to vibrate on totally different frequencies and become invisible to earthly eyes!

Maybe this species doesn't even live on the surface but inside these planetoids. Perhaps they seldom materialize as we see them in the UFOs. Regardless, there are many signs that this population living hypothetically near Jupiter has attained a level of consciousness from which we should profit.

And if they live even further away, that speaks more for their high level of intelligence.

We can consider ourselves fortunate that a more highly developed culture wants to help our aggressive, unsettled world. Could it be an attempt to save us from ourselves?

It takes approximately 30 minutes light speed for a radio message from Earth to reach Jupiter and its moons (depending on their momentary distance). If we consider that our crop-circle ETs, who obviously have an advanced technical understanding, also have a way to detect any messages sent from Earth in any direction, then they might have received our letter immediately and might have decided shortly afterwards to call back by their chosen method. Crop circles started to appear in the late '70s and became more and more complex. Can we conclude that the ETs decided to contact us via increasingly complex circles or that they had to develop their chosen answering method over the years?

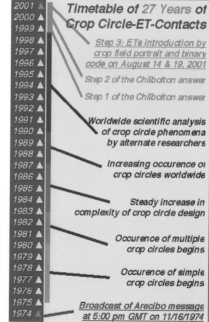

Timetable of 27 Years of Crop Circle-ET-Contacts

Year	
2001 ▲	Step 3: ETs introduction by crop field portrait and binary code on August 14 & 19, 2001
2000 ▲	
1999 ▲	
1998 ▲	
1997 ▲	
1996 ▲	
1995 ▲	Step 2 of the Chilbolton answer
1994 ▲	Step 1 of the Chilbolton answer
1993 ▲	
1992 ▲	
1991 ▲	Worldwide scientific analysis of crop circle phenomena by alternate researchers
1990 ▲	
1989 ▲	
1988 ▲	
1987 ▲	Increasing occurence of crop circles worldwide
1986 ▲	
1985 ▲	
1984 ▲	Steady increase in complexity of crop circle design
1983 ▲	
1982 ▲	
1981 ▲	Occurence of multiple crop circles begins
1980 ▲	
1979 ▲	Occurence of simple crop circles begins
1978 ▲	
1977 ▲	
1976 ▲	
1975 ▲	Broadcast of Arecibo message at 5:00 pm GMT on 11/16/1974
1974 ▲	

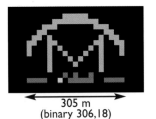

305 m
(binary 306,18)

Everyone was greatly surprised by the pixel structure at the bottom end of the alien answer. It is more than obvious that it is a miniature representation of the Butterfly Fractal of 2000, which was in the *same* field at the *same* place. This proves that the transmission method of the ETs is not coincidental, because this was the place in our message where the picture of the huge Arecibo telescope was placed. (The cosmic ET transmitter appears to be considerably larger.)

ET DIFFERENCE #9 & 10: TRANSMITTER & ITS SIZE

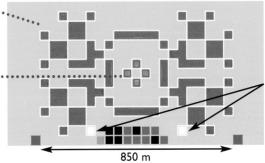

A simple mosaic pixelation processing of the Butterfly Fractal by computer shows clearly that ET meant its response to mirror our message.

The strange square cross at the position of Jupiter has been interpreted by some analysts as a mega-spaceship, but 12.7 billion passengers seems too many to me.

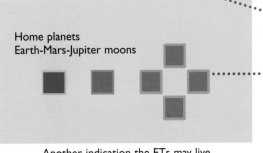

Home planets
Earth-Mars-Jupiter moons

Another indication the ETs may live on the moons of Jupiter.

These two pixels were intentionally left out by the ETs to leave room for the median measurement pixels.

850 m
(binary 67 x 12,6 = 850,25)

Better reception through grouping: 27 telescopes (each 23 yards wide) in a Y-configuration with a total width of 22 miles

saucer or space probe. Others think that the Butterfly refers to the two hemispheres of the brain and could, because of its mandala form, also be interpreted as an invitation to engage in telepathy. But because a figure for its size is written below the beamer instrument, I am in favor of a gross-material interpretation. I believe that the form of the transmission station in the crop formation is meant as a bird's-eye view. I have also modeled its fractal structure into three dimensions, creating possible side-views. (See illustrations on page 88.)

The operators of the VLA (Very Large Array) telescope in the deserts of New Mexico are already using, in a rudimentary way, the added power of antenna-dishes clustered in rows and triangle formations. We still have a lot to learn from ET.

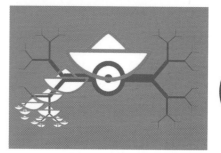

The central dish diameter is approximately 439 feet.

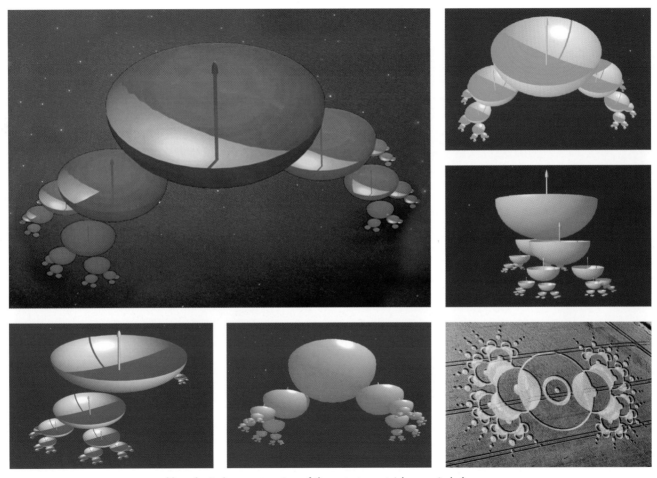

Hypothetical reconstruction of the extraterrestrial crop-circle beamer

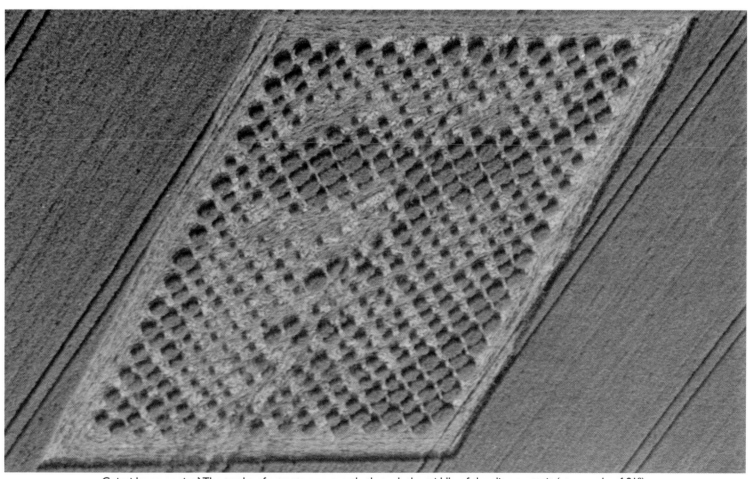

Coincidence or sign? The tracks of a tractor go exactly through the middle of the alien portrait (at an angle of 81°).

There have been numerous accounts of lights within and around crop circles, usually during or after their formation. Sometimes electrostatic and buzzing sounds have also been reported.

There are moving light balls visible on some videos and films and strange light-spots on some photographs. It seems that this light is guided by some intelligent system.

Similar to lightening balls, but not moving in such an illogical way, these glowing light balls move along certain lines or curves for seconds or minutes on the field — alone or in groups — along the top of the grain plants, then outside the circle, soon disappearing without a trace.

In June, 1999, a young man in the Netherlands was awakened by these magic balls before the creation of a crop circle. Looking out of his window, he could see two pink-purple light balls evolve spontaneously in his family's wheat field. The "BOLs" came in his direction before merging and producing two circles of 4- and 10-yard circumferences.

He was astonished to experience the same thing several nights later as a third, even larger, circle could be seen in the same field.

The "Diamond" of 1999, graphically enhanced for visibility

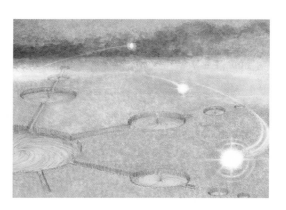

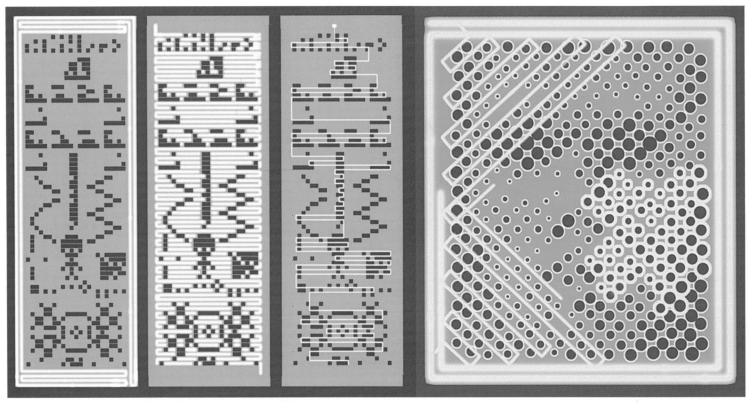

These are the most likely ways the different sized plasma balls moved through the field to fulfill their order. The BOLs seem to have started with the frame (there are unsubstantiated rumors a pilot saw a frame in the Chilbolton field in the early morning of August 14). If we consider the speed of these semi-transparent luminous spheres as captured on different crop-circle videos, they might have completed their job on the Chilbolton formations within just a few minutes.

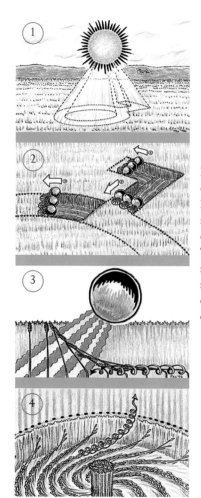

Beaming is the quantum-mechanical connection of billions of atoms. Bits of information, e.g., quantum-states, are transmitted by making copies of them at other places. This was also recently done to a small degree on Earth and will surely sooner (i.e., with ET's help) or later be possible over greater distances and with larger objects.

"We have formed crop circles using what Humans would call 'proto-plasmic ionic light rays.' Spheres of light made with biotechnological elements carry the data much like one of your 'copying' machines and transplant the image into the crop fields. Afterwards, the crop spheres merely disintegrate." — *Telepathic Transmission*

93

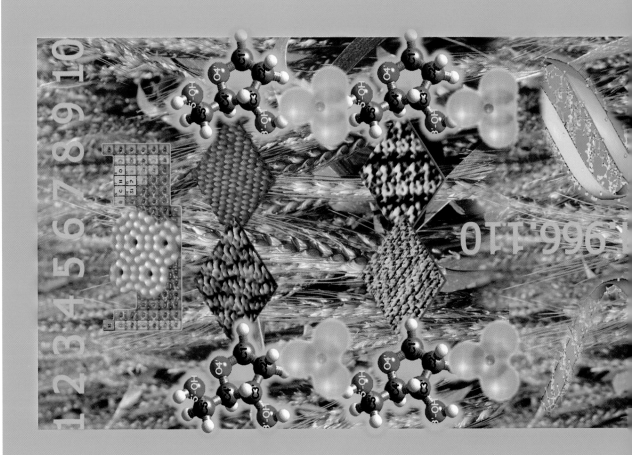

The proof that the crop correspondence is of alien origin can only come from direct contact with the circle-makers. But it seems that this communicating intelligence — perhaps because of their ethics — are awaiting a sort of earthly invitation rather than be considered unwanted intruders.

One thing is certain: It does not makes sense to wait for any governments to respond to these messages — at least not publicly. So it is better that we, the people of Earth, take the opportunity ourselves.

Since no one else is volunteering an answer, I have a suggestion how we all can and should answer collectively and globally.

As we are not yet able to beam our answer into the ice crust of moon Europa or onto the surface of one of the other Jupiter moons, and it is probably not helpful to make our next conversation a manmade crop formation in a grain field on Earth (which might not even be detected by ET), I believe we should develop three parallel approaches:

1) I think the best way — to be consistent and clear — is to use the same binary matrix employed by SETI in its original message and ET in its return call. Our answer should be transmitted once at the same frequency (2380 MHz), but does not need to be as powerful as the Arecibo transmission, as the distance to Jupiter is shorter.

2) At the same time we could also transmit a newly formatted 1679 beeps with the help of hundreds or even thousands of private shortwave radio stations during a designated period. Then there will be a greater chance that a complete set of signals will reach the intended addressee. Although this is merely a gesture to show our longing and intention of becoming members of a planetary federation, we will by this activity — and its coverage by the press worldwide — at the same time build up a sort of critical mass within the collective world consciousness (and change our distorted Hollywood-thriller-induced view of extraterrestrial beings).

Hello Jupiter
Message Day
worlwide interplanetary
telepathic communication
on February 1,2003

3) We could also attempt a more advanced contact via telepathy at a specific day for a specific time (let's say ten minutes at the top of each hour) around the world from each time zone. That way, there would be a whole day with an armada of telepathic messages sent to Jupiter. As this message has to be centered around an easily memorized logo, I propose an abstraction of the Earthly and alien script figures holding hands. That graphic is simple, emotional, and sends a clear message: LET'S BE FRIENDS!

Therefore I am herein personally proclaiming the HELLO JUPITER MESSAGE DAY on February 1st, 2003, because on this day the distance is closest between Earth and Jupiter.

Everyone is invited to participate and to help make our effort a success. With help from friends, I will launch a new Web site,

WWW.HELLOJUPITER.COM

where all necessary information will be placed, and the prepared chain of binary beeps of the answer I have designed can be downloaded either digitally or acoustically for use by anyone trying to broadcast them via radio communication.

The information on the site will be translated by volunteers into many different languages and spread all over the world via the Internet and any mass media willing to cooperate.

One thing is certain: To succeed at this tremendous task — beyond the scale of anything ever before — we need a lot of enthusiastic volunteers! I can only initiate and hopefully coordinate this extraordinary attempt. We also need sponsors who understand that the time for humanity to reach out has arrived. My vision is that "hello-groups" of all sizes form around the globe.

These groups can be coordinated both through the Web and local coordination centers, across all races and religions

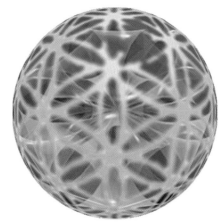

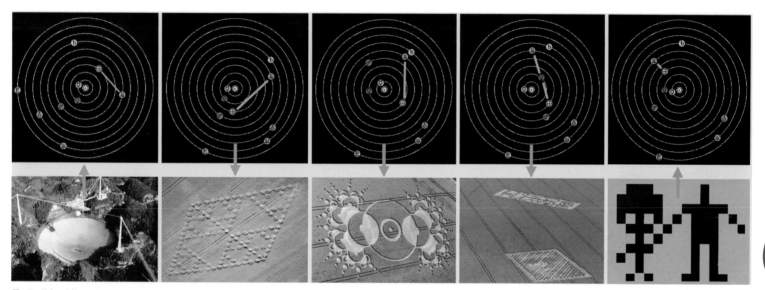

To "call back" at the symbolic date when Earth and Jupiter are closest should be the logical next step of the two-way communication already begun between us and the extraordinary intelligence in space.

worldwide. On February 1st, 2003, I foresee all these groups and individuals uniting mentally and/or spiritually by sending harmonious and peaceful thoughts of friendship to our cosmic neighbors in space, showing them with our telepathic mass mail that a relevant number of people on Earth are ready to shake hands. Even if you are skeptical, this is the day to cast your doubts aside. You have nothing to lose and so much to gain!

Before the three approaches above take place, I suggest we warn ET what is coming by transmitting a message via fractal antenna(s) from Earth to Jupiter from the end of this crop-circle season onwards at least once a week, announcing the January 31 date when the mass contact by hundreds of thousands of small transmissions and even more people communicating via telepathy will occur.

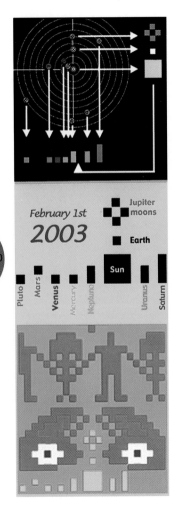

Here is my proposed (partly numerical and partly symbolic) message to ET:

On February 1st, 2003, we, the people of Earth, will attempt to contact you on Jupiter's moons to tell you we wish to be cosmic friends. In addition, we want you to know that we have understood the information hidden in the proportions of the crop circle face, where the star tetrahedron, the most basic structure of the universe, gives birth to light in its center.

Think of it! How wonderful! On February 1st, 2003, we will not only establish a constellation of maximum closeness between ET's home and mankind's planet, we will also depict this momentous date by the abstract pixels used in both the Arecibo and the Chilbolton scripts! These planet pixels only have to be arranged in a new, easily decoded way as a special constellation within our solar system and therefore identified on this special date when Earth and Jupiter are closest!

To understand this, look at the heliocentric positions of the planets as shown in my illustrations. As the time of maximum closeness there is a straight row of the sun, Earth, and Jupiter in space — so we take this line as the vertical axis. Then, with our point of view from Jupiter to the rest of the planets, we can see them depicted in the different positions.

I have colored the telepathy part of the suggested radio message to explain it more clearly: The abovementioned abstracted constellation is embedded into a human forehead, depicted with two eyes and a third eye in the center, beside the left and the right hemispheres of the brain. This part of the depiction is the most difficult to decode, but I am sure that ET will have no problem understanding what this pixelated abstraction says: We are concentrating that day on the moons of Jupiter and sending the ETs our thoughts of friendship via telepathy.

The lower parts of our reply script are easily decoded: There is one bigger and several smaller radio dish abstractions which say that we will use a multitude of antennas to transmit our new message within our solar system. Our attempt is also emphasized by the connection between Earth and Jupiter in the double solar system depiction.

I think this plan is a good start to attempt to reach the next level of more direct communication and contact with 12.7 billion of our small circle-maker friends. Then, all we have to do is wait for the next grain harvesting season... if not before... for the response — and more history in the making.

The book of nature is written in the language of mathematics. Numbers control the universe and allow us to understand all of existence. It is numbers' task to explain reality to us. Zero is the opposite of infinite infinities. Every whole number is a prime number or a product of prime numbers.

The order in numbers can be shown in many ways. The decimal system is the most widespread way on Earth, but the binary system, made up of two elements, is the simplest. The power of computers is based on this dual system, in which only two states are known:

ON / OFF = ONE / ZERO = LIGHT / DARK

From this we can conclude: Optimal communication with someone with a totally different mental thought-structure should take place, if not directly by telepathy, at least by means of binary impulses arranged in a recognizably simple prime number matrix.

2 - 3 - 5 - 7 - 11 - 13 - 17 - 19 - <u>23</u> - 29 - 31 - 37

Prime numbers are whole numbers (except for the number 1 itself) which cannot be divided by any other whole numbers besides themselves and the number 1 (e.g., 2,3,5,7,11,13…).

James Jean pointed out in 1941 that one could best get the attention of intelligent Martians, if they exist, by means of the strongest search spotlights blinking in the sequence of the lower prime numbers. It has also been suggested that one can view the occurrence of prime numbers in extraterrestrial radio signals as evidence for their "artificial," i.e., intelligent, origins.

41 - 43 - 47 - 53 - 59 - 61 - 67 - 71 - <u>73</u> - 79

The first method of calculating prime numbers was developed by the ancient Greek scholar, mathematician, and geometer Eratosthenes of Cyrene (about 275 to 195 BC).

This brief excursion into the world of numbers is necessary in order to help you understand the reasons for, and the method of, constructing binary coded messages.

The ETs have correctly understood our graphic symbols as well as the mathematically coded ones, for they have placed the proper correlates in their answers at the exact same position of the matrix established by us in our question. In fact, they have used the limited possibilities of the given matrix to the greatest extent possible.

Our message to the stellar position of cluster M13 began with the description of the predominant numerical system on earth: coded in binary numbers (as it is done in the Internet), the numbers 1 to 10 of the decimal system being represented to the aliens in a binary form as pixels.

`0101110001101011011101010`

decimal ➤	binary ➤	abstract
0	0	
1	1	
2	10	
3	11	
4	100	
5	101	
6	110	
7	111	
8	1000	
9	1001	
10	1010	
11	1011	
12	1100	

`0010011001100010100111011`

Binary numbers distinguish themselves from our usual decimal numbers by being expressed as the sum of the powers of the base number 2.

This requires only the numbers 0 and 1. The value of a 1 depends on its position in the number: at position 1 it counts as 1, at position 2 as 2, at position 3 as 4, at position 4 as 8, etc. The only function of the 0 is as a digit-marker putting the 1 at the proper position. This can be shown in the table to the left:

It makes no difference whether the aliens read the matrix from left to right or vice versa. By positioning a stopper-pixel in front of each number the — partly two-lined (the numbers 8, 9 & 10) — mathematical message can be read in any case without effort.

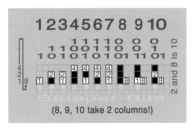

And it worked. In fact, the reply came back sooner than expected!

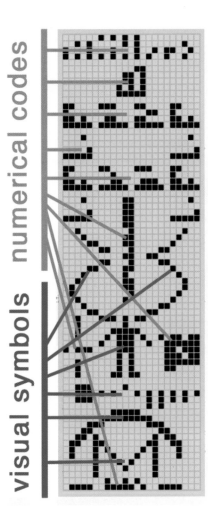

numerical codes

visual symbols

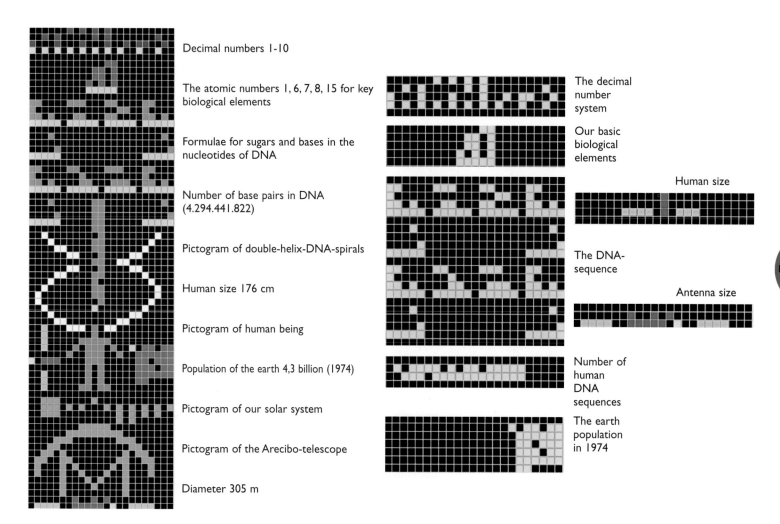

Decimal numbers 1-10

The atomic numbers 1, 6, 7, 8, 15 for key biological elements

Formulae for sugars and bases in the nucleotides of DNA

Number of base pairs in DNA (4.294.441.822)

Pictogram of double-helix-DNA-spirals

Human size 176 cm

Pictogram of human being

Population of the earth 4,3 billion (1974)

Pictogram of our solar system

Pictogram of the Arecibo-telescope

Diameter 305 m

The decimal number system

Our basic biological elements

Human size

The DNA-sequence

Antenna size

Number of human DNA sequences

The earth population in 1974

Sierpinski's Triangles

*The fractal design named after the Polish mathematician
Waclaw Sierpinski (1882-1969) was first described in 1916.*

It is the "self-similar" quality of this matrix that
makes it so interesting. Every triangle contains three smaller equilateral triangles, those
triangles again include three triangles, and so forth to infinity. This design has become a basic
function in fractal and chaos-theory. The Sierpinski Pyramid is derived from such a matrix in
three-dimensional form. These structures are also used to optimize antennas because they
resonate at any frequency. In a combination of electromagnetism and geometry, they are
utilized in mobile phones.

Sacred Geometry

*Form is just as inseparable
from geometry as geometry is
inseparable from vibration,
resonance, and frequency. In
other words: Every form has
an individual "consciousness."*

For eons mystics have known about the vibrating form of consciousness. Contemporary research in a
wide range of areas confirms that thoughts, emotions, and attitudes not only influence matter, but also
produce a type of sub-atomic strata upon which matter streams in recognizable patterns. Every change
in feeling or mood, even the tiniest nuance, influences the whole by means of geometry. "Sacred
Geometry" is the doorway to the principle of all-unity, indivisibility, and imminent oneness of creation.

Sound is form. For example, the chanting of the holy syllable OM by Tibetan monks was recorded and
transmitted to a resonance-plate covered with sand-crystals. The vibrating sand immediately took the
shape of the Sri Yantra — according to Hindu tradition, the pattern of the creation of the universe.

The five new theorems Euclid had not found.

Renowned mathematician Gerald S. Hawkins discovers new geometrical theorems within crop circle structures.

Mathematical analysis of the crop formation phenomenon has yielded insights about an intellectual profile involved in the creation of the crop patterns. It is either human-inspired or a completely independent intelligence whose intentions are not yet understood.

Gerald Hawkins began studying the geometries after a career as chairman of the Astronomy Department at Boston University. He co-authored the book *Stonehenge Decoded*, which hypothesized that Stonehenge marked sacred astronomical occasions such as solstices and equinoxes when sun or moon was framed in the archways.

Dr. Hawkins discovered five new intriguing theorems embedded in a lot of geometrical crop patterns and not found in Euclid or modern day geometry texts. Interviewed by investigative reporter Linda Moulton Howe, here is a condensed version of his view:

Friends and colleagues asked me what was behind it all, because crop circles were occurring near Stonehenge, and they wondered if there was some mysterious connection.

Crop circles are a phenomenon of the end of the 20th Century and the media were all opting for hoaxers as the cause, so I decided to investigate the hoax theory. I have a fairly broad background in astronomy, mathematics, physics and radio astronomy, but even more fortunately — as you will see — I am my wife's harp tuner.

My approach was to study the intellectual profile behind the patterns, as it turned out to be an even greater mystery than the mechanics of how they are formed. I was not very successful in proving the hoax theory; however, I made some important discoveries along the way.

I found the circles contained musical information, new mathematics, and even a code which, by statistical analysis, has a high confidence level of intentionality. The circle sizes gave numbers which matched diatonic ratios, which are the step-ups in pitch of the white notes of the piano.

I found two simple rules in the crop formations. First, for satellite patterns and separated circles, you divide the large diameter by the smaller. Second, for concentric rings and shapes, you divide the outer area by the inner. We began to see the geometries as unembellished, rotationally symmetric diagrams based on four theorems: circles were placed so that if a tangent were drawn between them, they made the theorem. But these creations were new mathematics — although being simple geometric shapes with outer and inner concentric circles — following on from where Euclid left off and not to be found in modern textbooks. Each one gave diatonic ratios corresponding to notes in the octave, C D E F G A B.

The fifth theorem was found by Gerald Hawkins within the Litchfield formation of 1995.

For the mathematically-minded, the areas of the circles give whole number ratios. With regular polygons, only the triangle, square, and hexagon give diatonic ratios, and only these shapes were used by the circle makers in the formative period till 1993. In the triangle, the area of the outer circle divided by the inner is 4, and the annular rings give 3. In the square, the ratio is 2 and the hexagon is 4/3. For the musically-minded, those numbers give C (3) in the third octave, G (2), and first octave F.

Thus, three points on the circle-makers' intellectual profile seemed to be visual, mathematical, and musical. I had also found a fifth theorem, which was the starting point for the other four. I wondered if the "unidentified hoaxers" also knew this, so I kept it to myself. *Science News and Mathematical Teacher* readers were trying to guess it, but no one succeeded. Whether or not the circle designers read those magazines is a moot question because they did show knowledge of the fifth theorem in the so-called Celtic Torc at Litchfield in July 1995. This 200-foot formation was accurately surveyed, and the geometry fit to within inches.

The fifth theorem stated that when a triangle is drawn with the sides touching concentric circles, then as the triangle changes shape, the areas of the circles make the ratios of musical intervals. When the triangle is isosceles with two sides equal, it will generate the square and hexagon by rotation. The fifth diagram is unusual because the diagram moves, pulsing in and out, changing shape as on a computer screen.

Even though my work is straight scientific research, it has been difficult to budge my colleagues. Perhaps they fear to tread into a subject beclouded with fringe speculations, or perhaps their background is not broad enough.

Doug and Dave said they made circles "for a laugh," so we could not match the intellectual profile with those two hoaxers. Interestingly, none of the few hoaxers have shown any interest in what I have found. Fortunately, no latter-day hoaxers could alter what took place in the formative period of 1981-1993. That data was safely sealed in a time capsule, beyond challenge. From my point of view, like the astronomy at Stonehenge, which was set in stone, the mind behind the phenomenon was in the record, set in the wheat.

I have proved crop circles can't be a natural phenomenon like whirlwinds, lightning, or unguided plasmas. Furthermore, that intellectual profile is unique, touching the history of mathematics from Euclid to fractals and music from Pythagoras to English church bells. If the phenomenon is transcendental, our culture is not currently prepared to face such a possibility; but if it is transcendental, then future society is in for a profound shock.

Condensed and reprinted from the book Mysterious Lights and Crop Circles, with permission from the author, Linda Moulton Howe

APPENDIX II
THE SETI
DRAMA

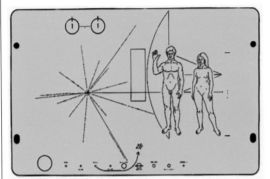

FURTHER ATTEMPTS OF
EARTHLINGS TO MAKE CONTACT

1972/74: The gold plaque of
PIONEER 10 & 11

1977: The gold-plated record of
VOYAGER 1 & 2

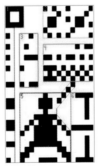

The first version,
which was not used

Astronomer Carl
Sagan was one of
the originators of
the earthly binary
message.

THE SEARCH FOR
EXTRATERRESTRIAL INTELLIGENCE

SETI began in the 1960s through the cooperation of many institutions and individuals. Hundreds of millions of dollars have been invested since.

The idea of transmitting a message to a distant star-cluster approximately 24,000 light-years away from Earth was admittedly conceived as a publicity gag by SETI managers, who were under public pressure to justify their expenditures. Ostensibly this message was meant to publicize the re-opening of the technically-improved Arecibo telescope with the motto: "No answer could ever come back before the year 51974 anyway!"

Now some SETI members may be embarrassed to discover ETs closer to home have taken the initiative, and that other senders are stealing their show!

At any rate, SETI seems to have now launched a counter-attack with a new motto: "The show must go on!" To keep up the appearance of "inviting ET to tea," they are getting millions of computer owners to join their bandwagon by downloading a screensaver that uses those computers when they are "at rest."

On August 19, 2001, SETI's house of cards collapsed. Their reaction: It cannot be true; in fact, we cannot believe or even think of admitting it could be true.

A few days after the Chilbolton appearance, SETI announced, without close investigation, that what had happened was a huge swindle. They claimed that there was no sign of any extraterrestrial source for the answer formation, and their Web site propagated a shallow argument featuring five points, which we will discredit, as follows:

Seth Shostak, speaker of the self-instituted quasi-official earthly contact ministry

SETI POINT #1: "Why would the ETs resort to an extraordinarily crude method of replying by carving simple messages in our wheat?.... If radio isn't their thing, why don't they simply leave a copy of the Encyclopedia Galactica on the doorstep of either the farmer or the radio observatory?..."

REBUTTAL TO #1: It is rather foolish to imagine that a more highly developed alien civilization wouldn't know how to best approach a more primitive one. Anyway, the alien message only mirrors the level of complexity offered by the SETI message.

SETI POINT #2: "How come they look like us? Hollywood aliens always look pretty humanoid, but this is anthropocentric conceit...."

REBUTTAL TO #2: It is silly to have ever thought ET must look completely different from us. On the contrary, it would be rather strange if life everywhere in the universe were completely different, for the same basic chemistry building blocks seemingly exist everywhere in space.

SETI POINT #3: "The Arecibo beam is about two arc-minutes... that's extremely narrow. The chances that it has hit another solar system in the 27 years since its broadcast are approximately 1:50.000!"

REBUTTAL TO #3: There are so many arguments against this point, there is not enough space to list them all. Thousands of UFO sightings and the transmissions of earthly TV programs (including the Arecibo message) up to 50 light-years into space should be sufficient evidence.

Also, SETI is concealing the fact that the original message of 1974 has been sent three more times by the "Cosmic Call" Project on June 30 and July 1, 1999, from the 70m-radiotelescope Evpatorya in Crimea, Ukraine, under the name "Encounter 2001." Four nearby stars roughly 60 light-years distant were targeted.

SETI POINT #4: "Keep in mind that of the hundreds of possible amino acids, only twenty are used for earthly life. In other words, our biochemistry is somewhat specific. How curious (and unlikely!) that theirs would match ours so closely!"

REBUTTAL TO #4: This logic is simply bad science, if science at all. What if, for instance, these ETs belong to the genetic forefathers of earthly mankind, a theory held by many alternative scientists?

SETI POINT #5: "The whole matter fails the baloney test. Why would aliens resort to a signaling system that conveys so little information... that can be easily made by people interested in creating a stir?...There is a lack of convincing physical evidence that anyone else has made them!"

REBUTTAL TO #5: Yes, there have been some counterfeit crop circles. There is, however, enough evidence to show that a hyper-technology yet unknown to us is being used here!

STICKING YOUR HEAD IN THE SAND WILL NOT CHANGE THE FACTS!

There is only one cosmological conclusion: We have come into contact with a species more advanced in its evolution, and it is tapping us lightly on the shoulder.

The background of the SETI Arecibo transmission revealed:

"It was strictly a symbolic event, to show that we could do it," explained Donald Campbell, at that time a research associate and now a professor of Astronomy at Cornell University (the administrators of the project), at the 25th commemoration of the Arecibo transmission.

"Nobody has called back yet, but that's okay, we weren't really expecting an answer.... The real purpose of our message was to call attention to the tremendous power of the newly installed radar transmitter....But many of those present took the event seriously because we translated the radio-frequency message into a warbling audio tone that was broadcast over speakers at the ceremony," says Harold Craft, at that time director of the observatory and today a vice president at Cornell.

In many crop circles, even the smallest details have been recognized as important!

Which hidden references are there in this most unusual crop sign? And why has this information been so cleverly hidden?

If we consider the left side of this photo, we can make these observations:

1) Although there was enough space, the four corner pixels are missing, leaving open both ends of the top and bottom (a total of 30) lines of the matrix.

2) The frame is not only supposed to improve the appearance of the picture. It also has a specific breadth, which is also probably important.

3) The contour of the middle tractor track goes directly through the middle of the picture.

4) Under the picture itself there are several unusual rings visible in the grain.

5) The left edge of the frame is exactly pointed at the operations building of the telescope.

6) The proportions of the whole picture probably are significant.

APPENDIX IV
THE
INVISIBLE
WATERMARK

The low angle of the sun in the morning causes the slightly irritating shade behind each of the 412 grain-matrix dots, the biggest 3 yards in diameter!

These are not the usual proportions of our passport photos.

They are also not formed to fit the proportions of ET's head, because his forehead is obviously cut off.

What then are these proportions meant to show us?

The same photo processed to show the exact view from above (the tractor tracks are now parallel).

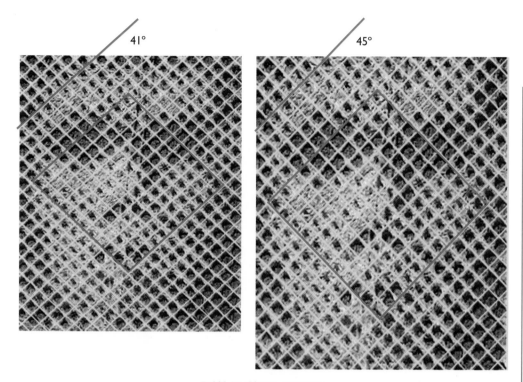

41°   45°

DOT MATRIX ANGLES

HALFTONE-PRINTING

A half-tone matrix reduces graphic information down to the essentials. The individual pixels or matrix-dots lying between the intersections of the matrix-lines produce together by their individual formal imprint more or less spatial depth and more or fewer half-tones — depending on the pixel size. The degree of contrast therefore depends on the proximity, the width, the angle of the lines, the pixel form, and the background.

At first glance one would think that the face with a stubbly beard is in a 45° matrix. It is only upon reconstructing the 30 dotted lines (woven crosswise) that one discovers that it is an approximately 41° matrix (the later-calculated exact measurement was 40.89°). This again underlines the obvious importance of the proportions, which are meant to make us aware of something. I asked the British researcher Charles Mallett for his measurements made on the spot (see page 115).

A matrix-point
measures about
three yards.

Mallett had only made measurements of one horizontal and one vertical edge of each of the two objects, but he believed he had exact measurements with a margin of error of perhaps 1-2 feet:

THE FACE: 145 x 165 feet = 44,2 x 50,3 m
THE CODE: 90 x 265 feet = 27,4 x 80,8 m

With these numbers I could estimate the proportions to be at least 1:1.14 and modify the scanned pictures accordingly. The above-mentioned details became apparent and I began to investigate the background further. It was helpful that I had just recently translated a book on Sacred Geometry (see page 104). I drew a parallel line from the most mysterious point to the tractor tracks, mirroring them also to the left side. At some point it occurred to me to connect various crossing lines and was soon astounded at the cosmic secret hidden in ET's portrait!

Here are the small "key" points to the first hidden geometric formula. Later I also found the meaning of the two bigger "construction hints."

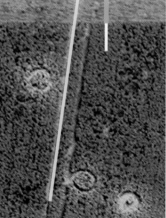
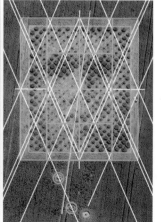

The junctions of the upper and lower picture edges with the left and right lines (in red) drawn parallel to the middle tractor track (approx. 81° inclination) are connected by the purple line, which completed an equilateral triangle using the (blue) right-angle intersection on the base line as my axis.

When I discovered that the (green) diagonal of the rectangle containing this triangle was parallel to the grain-matrix, I knew that I was on the right path. (Ultimately this turned out to be the final test of my discovery. The further steps to complete the diagram are indicated by dots.)

I then mirrored the triangle several times, gradually coming closer to the solution. Through the (green) diagonal between the (white) outer rectangle corners, i.e., the triangle apexes, I could first measure and then calculate the mathematically exact proportions:

145 x 167.4 feet, that is only 7 feet longer than measured in the field! Besides, there is another way I proved the found proportions: As the exact proportions of the code-answer are known from the binary pixel structure plus frame — as the face is in the same field and photograph — one has only to rectify the code (together with the face) on a computerized photograph to obtain an exact bird's-eye view and then to measure the proportions of the face via computer.

All these trials and errors took several days, during which I was motivated to continue by the enticing stare of this being's deep eyes. Besides, I had been fascinated for years by the archaic knowledge of the ancient geometers.

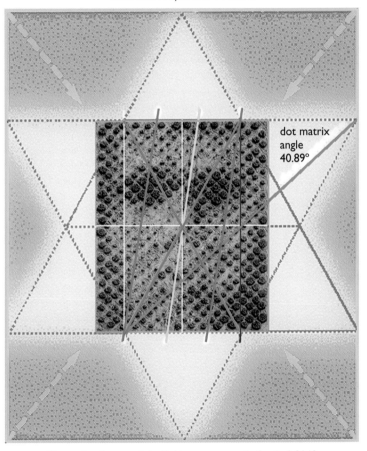

Horizontal Proportion 1 : 1,1547

dot matrix angle 40.89°

Correction factor of the field measurement of only 0,0168

Afterwards, it seems so simple and easy to explain. It was clear that hexagonal structures were the key, but what was the aim? Since the matrix portrait was the crown jewel among all the crop signs, I hoped to find some coded content within it.

From the discovery of the circumscribed hexagram to the exact fitting of this "Seal of Solomon" (as this ancient sign is also named) into the picture was a logical step. In fact, it was now apparent why the picture frame had its exact proportions: When a circle is drawn around the inner hexagram, it forms an exact tangent with the inner limit of the upper and lower frame sides and the outer limit of the left and right sides of the frame. The width of the frame itself is also proof of the correct proportions, as it can only have the width it really has in the field, and none else embrace the embedded secrets.

The solution of the extraterrestrial puzzle lies in the invisible "watermark hexagram," a symbol for universal knowledge in its oldest form, which had often been beamed by ET in many crop circles.

Indeed, whoever still believes in an earthly counterfeit of the Chilbolton transmission is beyond help. It is also ludicrous to believe that some military secret services are testing their weapons in the fields, as some non-believers have suggested.

The findings presented here still only scratch the surface of the cosmic know-how imbedded in the hexagon seal. The mouths of those who are allowed — on the basis of the higher frequency of their consciousness — to enter into these esoteric secrets will fall open in astonishment. A world which can raise itself into such spiritual dimensions can enjoy possibilities of which the majority of those on Earth today cannot even imagine.

The primacy of the spirit over matter — the real creative potential of man — together with this knowledge will change our lives greatly in the not too distant future. But a change in the political landscape of the world will be necessary. As long as it is the single egoistic and short-sighted goal of those in power to subordinate all other interests to remaining in power, ET & Co. will not think of sharing their know-how (e.g., in the field of free-energy propulsion systems) in a concretely usable form.

THE GREAT SYMBOL OF SOLOMON

A coded UFO-construction plan based on Pythagoras's Tetractys

Side-length of the cube : Radius of surround sphere = 1,1547005383007925

Apex-edge-length:
Radius of intermediate sphere
= 1,1547005383007925

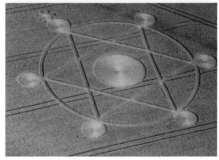

←—The breadth of the frame is set by the constructed surrounding circle.

When I was working on the British edition of my findings, I discovered the reason for the two still mysterious dots in the grain below the face. This was a real challenge to me; I could not give up until I found the cause of these strange details.

The other two construction points show the grid of the diamond fractal and the hexagram watermark based on the outer limit of the frame. Interestingly, the sizes of the construction points (seen at the bottom of the middle image) are the same as the biggest and the smallest face pixel dots.

THE HEXAGRAM

The ancient symbol of two overlapping triangles represents, in general, polarity itself and in particular: the interaction between the visible and the invisible worlds, the unity of the spiritual and the material realms and of personality and impersonality.

The origin of the hexagram can be found in the cosmos itself, whose matrix it forms — microscopically as well as macroscopically ("as it is above, so it is below; as it is inside, so it is outside"). The oldest mention of the hexagram was found in Hindu Tantra, where it was used as a symbol for sexual union: the triangle pointing downward represented the female, that pointing upward the male, with the sun in the center. This six-pointed star is sometimes also known as the Shield of David or the Seal of Solomon. (The Song of Solomon in the Bible hints at the fact that he was enlightened by a "Sacred Marriage," i.e., "Unio Mystica.")

In fact, hidden in different corners of the image of the face are the fundamentally fractal structure of the manifested world itself. Although it is embedded in a two-dimensional image, the message is clearly meant to be three-dimensional.

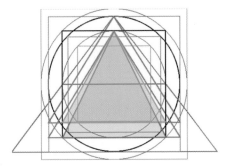

Although I am no mathematician, I discovered the different coded triangles must also connect with the old riddle of "squaring the circle."

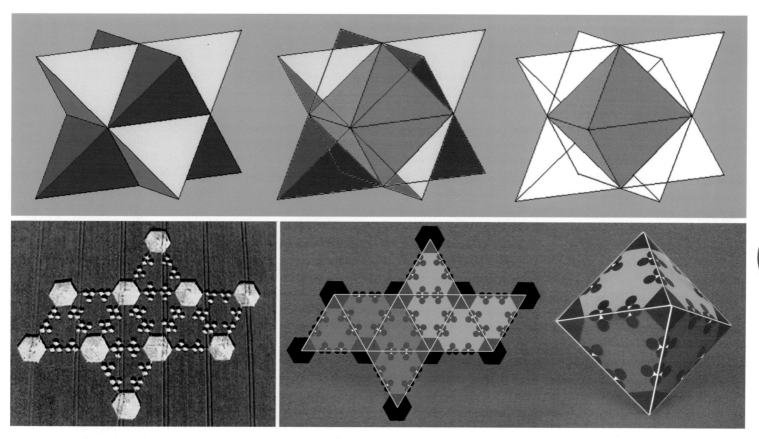

As early as 1999 at West Overton, the circle-makers showed us their secret with a fold-up pattern for the octahedron within which the core of the star-tetrahedron dwells.

The proportions in
the field (measuring
90 x 267 feet)
transposed into the
proportions of the
binary message (23 x
73 pixels plus frame)
show the contours
somewhat better —
without the distor-
tions caused by
shading in the
grain-field.

The 2 pixel-wide
frame of the message
was obviously
extended by ET by 2
further pixels at the
top and the bottom
to give a further clue
of "three" by dividing
the code-frame
lengths into exactly
three (face) parts
(81 : 27 = 3).

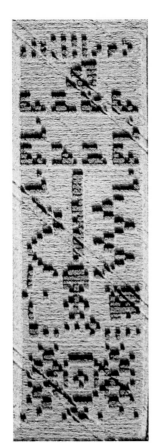

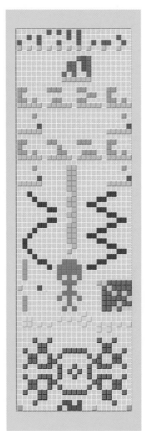

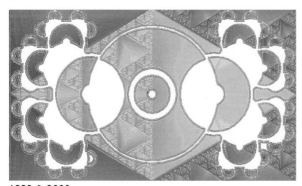

1999 & 2000

1999 & 2001

AN ABUNDANCE OF SIGNS

Doubling the proportions of all the fractal Chilbolton formations from 1999-2001 shows that all Chilbolton signs are mathematically identical!

2000 & 2001

All signs have invisible hexagramatic structures.

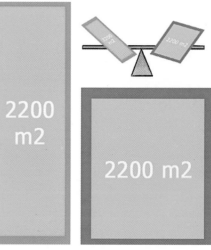

Even the area of both the script and the face are the same. Is ET trying to tell us that the message and the messenger are one and the same?

SILICON

Even the crystal lattice of the silicon embedded in ET's genetic code forms a hexagram matrix.

The double tetrahedron or eight-pointed star — named "Stella Octangula" by Johannes Kepler in his studies on the "harmony of the spheres" — is the primordial principle of three-dimensional materiality.

Seen from a perfect bird's-eye view, the double tetrahedron solid casts an exact hexagramatic shadow.

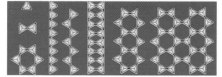

Schematic tetrahedonal structure of different silicates

By looking closely at the details of the Chilbolton formations, we should now clearly see that — especially in case of the face —the medium itself is quite literally the message. This pointillist grid, archetypically depicting the messenger who seemingly silently stares at us, is in fact speaking loudly. It is amazing that this androgynous being tells us some of the innermost secrets of creation without using any words— if only we have eyes to see and ears to listen. The possibility of communicating such deep truths by impressions in a grain field is extremely moving to me; otherwise I would have had neither the inspiration nor the energy to solve this riddle step by step.

During human history many wisdom seekers have found at least some of the spiritual secrets concerning how the material world came into being, although it was not always good for the health of the finder (e.g., Giordano Bruno, who was burned to death by the inquisition, or Hypanthia, who taught geometry at the library of Alexandria and was brutally killed for "witchcraft" by a Christian mob). Somehow in human history this knowledge periodically gets lost in the dark, and new wake-up calls have to be sounded to awaken the younger generations and inspire spiritual evolution.

APPENDIX VI
FURTHER
REFLECTIONS
FROM MY
SEARCH

126

Now again the time has come to dip into the blueprints of life. For what is a more appropriate response to the extraordinary "field demonstrations" with immense images that span and unite the realms of the physical with the meta-physical?

A contemporary scientist who is knocking at the doors of eternal wisdom is Rupert Sheldrake. In his revolutionary book *A New Science of Life*, he presents a new "hypothesis of formative causation" involving so-called morphogenetic fields. He discovered that "specific morphogenetic fields are responsible for the characteristic form and organization of systems at all levels of complexity," that is, biology, chemistry, physics — and also meta-physics, the subtle structured order behind the physical. "These fields order the systems with which they are associated by affecting events which, from an energetic point of view, appear to be indeterminate or probabilistic. They impose patterned restrictions on the energetically possible outcomes of physical processes. If morphogenetic fields are responsible for the organization and form of material systems, they must themselves have characteristic structures," which easily act across space and time. Sheldrake calls this process "morphic resonance." In layman's terms, thoughts create a resonance in the universe that affects actions in time and space. Since crop circles are geometrical thought patterns, they too resonate. As a real prayer is a means of creating a morphic resonance within one's mind, crop formations are vibrating temporary temples, healing us globally on a collective subconscious level to a more awakened state of experience of what life is really about.

These vibrations are part of the cosmic energy matrix, which is the true essence of all creation. Since crop circles are sort of "archaic mathematical thoughts," they can manifest beyond light speed — instantly and everywhere. No creation has ever come into being without being preceded by some of these building-block patterns of our reality.

The geometrically-coded universal matrix within which all things exist is analogous to the east's "unseen ground of existence." This subtle quasi-crystalline structured matrix is vibrationally alive on many orders of magnitude, the finest possibly a thousand times smaller than the smallest subatomic particle. Some modern theoretical physicists even have postulated the existence of a subquantic structered medium. This realm where seemingly all cellular autonomous processes and energetic functions are created has been named the "primordial ether" by Wilhelm Reich (a genius of the 20th century, who was said to be murdered for his findings by the CIA in 1957). There dwells the basic energy of life (called "orgon" by Reich), which animates the more physical realms. On this level also ESP and other paranormal actions first take place, before they are realized in the more dense dimensions of experience.

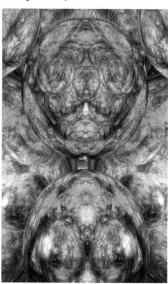

In fact, there is an underlying geometrical giga-grid with enormous structures and its ultra-tiny order of, let's say, "intentional grain" within the very ground of existence. Instead of an empty space, which still most of our earthly scientists believe in, we have a highly structured matrix of high energy and high information content. That means there is a total interconnectedness of all things. The medium is inside of and outside of all things. It is an interstellar medium and, in last consequence, the medium itself is all things. Seemingly evolved life forms have found ways at using this structured medium to enhance their creative abilities, e.g., to move within the universe and between dimensions with or without UFOs, and to draw circles or more complex formations into distant crop fields on other planets from afar.

So what is this geomatrix? To use physicist David Bohm's perfect terminology: "It is the ultimate implicate order from which the explicit order unfolds." Interestingly, the word matrix comes from *mater*, mother or "womb." In today's science it is defined as a) an intercellular substance, b) a place or surrounding substance within which something originates or develops, and c) something that gives form, foundation, or origin to something else enclosed in it. This polyhedral structure which fills all space from micro- to macrocosm with its multifaceted hexagramatic grid and its imminent intelligence can be considered as the universal primordial womb of the "universal mother" who gives birth to all thinkable things.

American scientist/artist Charles R. Henry has indeed proven that abstract geometrical structures are the basic order of the specific embryonic form in which life takes shape in its first stages.

This grand unifying theory of everything which physicists have been searching for is so very simple yet grandiose! It is the universal multifaceted matrix, the blueprint which underlies all creation at every stage of development, wherein the more dense building blocks of life have to follow like an architect's plans. Knowing this, we can perceive that it is not merely the crop fields themselves but the morphic fields *behind or between* the same spaces into which these sacred circles and fascinating formations are manifested. It seems to be more of a sort of acupuncturing of the very basic archaic morphic matrix with specific geometric structures which not only can be seen and enjoyed but which also — with their "organizational waves" — themselves induce new specific morphogenetic fields which have the ability to grow and develop like organisms on a higher vibratory level and even within the unconscious of the human mind. That is why Feng Shui and other wisdom teachings on how to create wholesome and supportive spaces in accordance with the laws of nature work well. On that same subtle level, healing systems like homeopathy and radionics are effective.

Crop circles have a healing potential as they reprogram millions of distorted energy patterns by "broadcasting" the healthy, holistic, original vibrational signatures within key points of the earthly energy grid. Call them planetary charkas, if you like. They activate transmission centers within the subtle energy field of our home planet to become more receptive for energies from supra-physical dimensions. Unmanifested God energy this way comes into form and in the long run is able to transform the stuck belief systems of our society. That is why they are still ignored by the dominant (unconsciously frightened) orthodox, mechanistic, and materialistic science and merely are being joked about by the mass media. But this will change. In the end we will laugh about our so-called High-Tech of today, which is nothing more than horrible, primitive Low-Tech hidden under polished covers (e.g., moving our bodies with cars by utilizing little explosions induced by gasoline).

Sacred Geometry is sacred because it is a description of the spiritual creation of the world. It is nothing less than a metaphor of the universal order and the wisdom of the way in which the universe is designed, and how spirit integrates into matter. It tells us the steps the spirit takes from pure energy into matter to create our physical bodies, the plants and animals, the planets, stars, solar systems, galaxies, and universes. Sacred Geometry fields which give birth into matter are around every natural thing and being. Ancient times always believed that the language of God is mathematics. Pythagoras himself said: "The essence of the cosmos is number." The hexagram was called "the form of the form" by the Pythagoreans. In alchemy the triangle tells of the threefold nature of God, and the eight-pointed star also represents the philosopher's stone. In Hinduism the same is symbolized by Trimurti of Brahma, Vishnu, and Shiva, and within their mathematical meditation images called yantras. Also, Buddhism emphasizes the great impact which mandalas have to the human psyche. In the western world, the great psychoanalyst Carl Jung is known for having done intense research on that theme. In 1619 Johannes Kepler states in *Harmonices Mundi* that "geometry is even before the creation of things, eternal like the spirit of God itself." Geometry first has shaped the archaic images necessary for the creation of the world. In its simplest form this energy field is a star tetrahedron which surrounds our human body and in ancient texts is referred to as Merkaba.

Giordano Bruno called the natural force between mathematics and physical things "mathesis," a sort of meta-mathematics. His drawings show great similarity with the basic grids of the crop circles of today.

All in all, it is the archaic morphic structure of endlessly-interlocked platonic solid grids in all dimensions which hold the world together. So it is no longer necessary to find a "world formula" for everything, as it simply lies before our eyes. We have only to adapt this imminent yet esoteric wisdom into our lives and into applicable everyday knowledge. Then it is not illogical to build UFOs and other anti-gravitational devices and to program light balls to create crop circle imprints into far away fields ourselves.

But beware: Although this higher intelligence is giving us a helping hand, it will not allow us to play creator with these advanced toys as long as Earth's population is not mature enough to handle them wisely. It needs to awaken at least a critical mass of consciousness, some percent of humanity, to get evolution to make this quantum leap.

If you think that all of this theorizing is a bit much for you, then let me end by citing the Nobel prize winner of physics, Max Born, who emphasized that "the metaphysics of one era is the science of the next."

PLAQUE OF HONOR OF CC-RESEARCHERS

Steve Alexander - Werner Anderhub - Paul Andersen - Colin Andrews - Ken Bakeman - Francine Blake - Dustin D. Brand - Toni Caldicott (†) - Brian L. Crissey - Zef Damen - Pat Delgado- Stuart Dike - Karen Douglas - Fintan Dunne - Mark J. Fussell - Julian Gibsone - Michael Glickman - Eltjo. H. Haselhoff - Michael Hesemann - Richard Hoagland - ilyes - Bert Janssen - Palden Jenkins - Andrew King - Joachim Koch - Ulrich Kox - Frank Laumen - William C. Levengood - Charles & Frances Mallett - Linda Moulton-Howe - Andreas Müller - Lucy Pringle - Hans Peter Roth - Keith Rowland - Red Setter - Ed & Kris Sherwood - J. Sherwood - Freddy Silva - Peter R. Sorensen - Robert Speight - Nancy S. Talbott - Busty Taylor - Paul Vigay - Randy Wiggins - Steve Wingate - and many more...

130

CROP CIRCLE WEB SITES & LITERATURE

There are now more than 1000 Web sites about crop circles and countless publications.

The most famous Web site is: www.cropcircleconnector.com

The biggest free database is at www.cropcircleresearch.com

You can find a lot of useful links at www.mysteries-megasite.com/cropcircles/crop.html

Also worth a look:
www.cosmicreflections.com (very aesthetic)
www.bltresearch.com (very scientific)
www.kornkreise.de/uk (very German)
www.kornkreise.ch (very Swiss)
www. Zef-damen.myweb.nl (very constructive)
www.swirlednews.com (very profound)

Some of the newest crop circle books for both beginners and advanced:

Andy Thomas
(www.vitalsignspublishing.co.uk)
Vital Signs — A Complete Guide to the Crop Circle Mystery and Why It Is Not a Hoax
Seaford, 2002, Revised Edition, S.B. Publications

Linda Moulton-Howe (www.earthfiles.com)
Mysterious Lights and Crop Circles
New Orleans, 2002, Updated Edition, Paper Chase Press

Freddy Silva (www.lovely.clara.net)
Secrets in the Fields — The Science and Mysticism of Crop Circles
Charlottesville, 2002, Hampton Roads Publishing

Eltjo H. Haselhoff (www.dcocc.com)
The Deepening Complexity of Crop Circles
Berkeley, 2001, Frog Ltd.

You will also find some of the best photographs, postcards, calendars, videos, CDs, magazines, catalogs, and yearbooks of crop circles at the Web sites of:

Lucy Pringle
(http://home.clara.net/lucypringle),
Steve Alexander
(www.temporarytemples.co.uk),
Colin Andrews (www.cropcircleinfo.com)

The Wiltshire Crop Circle Study Group — at whose Crop Circle Conference 2002 I gave my first lectures about the Chilbolton findings — presents a monthly crop formation newsletter called "The Spiral."

SPECIAL RECOMMENDATION:
Bruce A. Rawles (www.intent.com)
Sacred Geometry Design Sourcebook
Nevada City, 1997, Elysian Publishing

William Gazecki, *Crop Circles: The Quest for Truth.* Two-Hour Documentary Film, Released 2002

RULES FOR ENTERING CROP CIRCLES

If you have discovered a crop circle or want to visit an already discovered one, you should abide by the following rules:

1) If you believe yourself to be the first or one of the first to have discovered the formation, you should try to photograph the field from as high an angle as you can, if possible from the air (a bird's-eye view).

2) Note the geographic position on the basis of a drawing or mark a map accordingly (including nearest town, latitude, longitude, direction of formation, date, hour, type and maturity of crop).

3) Inform the owner before you enter the field — otherwise it could amount to trespassing.

4) Enter the field only over previous tractor tracks, never wade through the standing crops. Enter even the flattened areas of the formation only with care.

5) Take pictures of or draw as many details as possible. Look out for unusual signs and/or signs of possible fake formations (e.g., holes in the ground, only broken stalks...). Note your psychic reaction.

6) Jot down/make a drawing of the pictogram, adding also the position and rotation angle of the bent stalks. Inquire about possible time of origin and ask local people about their observations.

7) Request the owner to leave the crop standing, if possible, for further investigation (e.g., surveying, sample collection).

8) Report your discovery to the nearest crop circle center.

9) Do not enter the field at all in rainy weather, unless you are a researcher. Never smoke in the field or enter with dogs! Do not park where you may disturb traffic, etc. Keep an eye on your children.

10) Remember that responsible corn-crop research is dependent on cooperation with farmers and act accordingly.

Thank you!

ABOUT THE AUTHOR

JAY GOLDNER, 51, is an Austrian graphic designer, author, and researcher in paranormal phenomena. A UFO-sighting twenty years ago while working on the geometric reconstruction of the Sri Yantra motivated him to extended studies in this area. He is planning to establish the world's first Crop Circle Museum in Austria. He has created many digital crop-circle paintings inspired by his research. He can be contacted via email: jaygoldner@nextra.at or at Studio Phoenix, P.O. Box 8, A-4810 Gmunden, Austria. www.hellojupiter.com

JUST BEFORE WE WENT TO PRESS: An amazing event has occurred on August 14, 2002. At the anniversary of the Chilbolton crop face and only eight miles from the telescope, a fascinating new formation has appeared in a wheat field: a huge figure of an alien drawn by 59 horizontal "TV lines" within a frame measuring 390 x 232 feet, along with a "mega data disc" with a 200-foot diameter. Inside this new crop circle is a data spiral with 17 windings that contain approximately 1,000 0 and 1 bits. Although the context is not yet decoded, the proportions of the image show the same hidden hexagram watermark as found in other circle art. So the mystery continues to unfold...